ORIG·7·93

370·113
FJN

VOCATIONAL EDUCATION
AND THE CHALLENGE OF EUROPE

NEW DEVELOPMENTS IN VOCATIONAL EDUCATION

Series Editors: Peter Funnell and Dave Müller

VOCATIONAL EDUCATION AND THE CHALLENGE OF EUROPE

RESPONDING TO THE IMPLICATIONS OF THE SINGLE EUROPEAN MARKET

PETER FUNNELL
DAVE MÜLLER

KOGAN
PAGE

To Sue, Simon and Rebecca
Vik, Lucy and Emily
for being there and being patient

First published in 1991

Kogan Page Limited
120 Pentonville Road
London N1 9JN

British Library Cataloguing in Publication Data
A CIP record for this book is available from the British Library.
ISBN 0 74940 127 3

Typeset by DP Photosetting, Aylesbury, Bucks
Printed and bound in Great Britain by
Clays Ltd, St Ives plc

Contents

Acknowledgements

We would like to express our thanks to all the colleagues and friends who have supported the production of this book. Particular thanks to: Sharon Smith, Graham Fox and those who contributed to the 'Challenge of Europe' series of national conferences organized by the Suffolk College between February 1989 and May 1990; Dolores Black at Kogan Page; and Deborah Whale and Anne McCrumlish for 'managing' the manuscript.

Series Preface

Currently enjoying renewed interest, vocational education has experienced substantial change during recent years in terms of its curriculum delivery and organization. It has faced up to the implications of the demographic downturn and is now responding positively to the challenge of the Single European Market and wider structural changes within Europe. The responsibility for vocational education is now shared more widely within the government between the Department of Education and Science and the Department of Employment. Changing government policy and practice during the 1980s has created an environment which is more competitive both between public sector institutions and private education and training providers.

The recognition that the United Kingdom has failed by European standards to provide sufficient training to meet employer needs has led to policies which aim to increase the participation rate for those aged 16 and over. The 1990s will witness the continuation and heightening of this process of change and the generation of new opportunities and challenges for those responsible for providing vocational education.

This series will focus on these opportunities and challenges. The aim will be to provide contemporary texts which focus on newly emerging issues in vocational education, with an emphasis on innovation. More specifically the series will seek to influence and inform practice by focusing on the application of new and original ideas. In this way the texts will be at the interface between theory and practice with the explicit intention of enabling practitioners and managers to apply new educational ideas and philosophies.

The books are designed for those engaged professionally in vocational education and will provide information on, and critical analyses of, new developments. The contemporary and applied nature of the series will furnish a valuable source of material on important current issues and will build into a library to illustrate the application of good practice. We hope you enjoy this and other texts in the series.

Peter Funnell and Dave Müller
Ipswich 1991

Foreword

Amadee Turner, Member of the European Parliament for Suffolk and South East Cambridgeshire

I am very pleased that Peter Funnell and Professor Dave Müller have taken the lead in exploring the relationship between vocational education and the new challenge of the Single European Market. It is a very great challenge, one so serious that it requires an immediate response which is both wide ranging and fully integrated. Certainly there is more to be done in Britain than among any of our equals in the European Community simply because our vocational education and training set-up is more rudimentary than theirs.

British industry and commerce has suffered from its relatively remote relationship with the world of vocational education. There are a number of reasons for this, an important one among these being the system and role of Chambers of Commerce in Britain as compared to, say, Germany or France. Whatever the reasons what is now needed is an immense push from those in vocational education to engage the full enthusiasm of business. This involves the very hard task of building bridges between commercial and educational objectives and practice. To achieve this, those in education and training will need to enlist the full support of local industrial and commercial leaders and local government.

However before anything can be done vocational educationalists and trainers will need to know what it is they should be offering and have an awareness of the markets they wish to serve. In this respect the experience of the authors as leaders of one of the earliest attempts to encourage a pro-active and entrepreneurial approach from vocational education to the Single European Market through a series of national conferences and seminars is important. This experience permeates the book while the text as a whole offers informed proposals and case-studies which by their obvious relevance and cogency seize the imagination. The world of vocational education should never be the same now that the Single

European Market is upon us. This book offers a valuable contribution to responding to the challenge of the Single European Market. I hope it succeeds in its task of familiarizing all those concerned with encouraging high-quality education with the implications of the Single European Market, and supporting British business to engage in successful competition with their equals on mainland Europe.

List of Contributors

Geoff Bemrose: Head of School of Science, Suffolk College, Ipswich

Brian Bonney   Project Director, Cambridgeshire 1992 Project, Cambridgeshire LEA

Christine Dobson   Principal, Ipswich School of Radiography

Mel Doyle   Assistant Secretary, Workers' Educational Association

Stefan Drew   Director of Enterprise, Isle College, Wisbech

Peter Funnell   Head of Faculty of Creative Studies, Suffolk College, Ipswich

Colin Hancock   UK Representative on the Economic and Social Committee of the European Community

Peter Luff   Director, European Movement

Frank McDonald   Course Leader, BA (Hons) Business in Europe, Manchester Polytechnic

Dave Müller   Vice Principal, Suffolk College, Ipswich

The Challenge of Europe – Assessing the Implications of the Single European Market

Introduction

The Single European Market and wider structural changes in Europe will have significant implications for vocational education in the United Kingdom (UK). These implications are likely to change over time but will ultimately have a profound effect on the post-16 curriculum and the teaching and learning styles and strategies employed to deliver it. This will, in turn, impact on the management of institutions offering vocational education and on the range of skills and competences required of the staff of these institutions.

At one level the implications of the Single European Market will produce a new set of challenges which will act as a drive towards the integration of a European dimension into the mainstream curriculum of vocational education. Additionally it will facilitate a restructuring of provision to make it attractive to the more explicitly European-focused client groups of the mid- and late 1990s. At a second level the implications of the Single European Market will intensify and give focus to a range of developments currently permeating the whole of vocational education. In particular those developments designed to:

- generate and extend the relevance of curricular provision and promote the development of a clear curriculum entitlement for students (Further Education Unit, 1989);
- promote greater responsiveness and commercialism in the operational practice of institutions offering vocational education, with sensitivity to market needs and demands encompassed in an often ill-defined concept of quality (Müller and Funnell, 1991);
- promote the application of a more entrepreneurial and business-orientated approach to the management of human, physical and financial resources within institutions and systems of vocational education.

In their respective chapters Peter Luff and Colin Hancock explore the broad implications of the Single European Market from the perspectives of senior commentators and practitioners in the field. Both acknowledge the enhanced competition generated by the Single European Market and the implications of this for existing and future levels of skill shortage, and more general areas of industrial and commercial practice in the UK.

In his chapter Luff identifies the Single European Market as part of a broader process towards greater political, economic, social and indeed cultural unity within the European Community. He criticizes the UK's insularity within Europe and points out the potentially detrimental impact of this on UK industrial and commercial practice in the 1990s. Luff offers a strong argument supporting a vocational educational response to the implications of the Single European Market both on economic grounds and as a precursor to the development of a more integrated Europe in the 1990s and beyond.

Hancock supports the view that the Single European Market will have significant social and economic implications for the UK. Hancock makes explicit the uncertainty surrounding predictions on the implications of the Single European Market: however he offers the view, supported by Luff, that on balance the economic benefits of the Single European Market will be positive for the UK, although unevenly spread.

This view differs in part from that offered by Rajan (Rajan, 1990) who suggests that the international process of large-scale capacity rationalization which has preceded the completion of the Single European Market, and is likely to continue throughout the 1990s, combined with skill shortages and the legacy of underprovision in vocational education, will leave the UK particularly vulnerable to enhanced economic competition. On this basis, he suggests, half the companies in Europe could disappear by the year 2000 and any economic gains during the first half of the 1990s resulting from the Single European Market will be modest. In summary this analysis suggests that there will be both commercial 'gainers' and 'losers' across the European Community as a consequence of the Single European Market with the UK at best 'breaking even' – enjoying the product of a 'zero sum game'.

However while there is uncertainty about the implications of the Single European Market for the UK economy as a whole, and individual regions and employment sectors therein, the impact of these changes on vocational education may be more clearly articulated.

Both Luff and Hancock are critical of the underprovision of vocational education in the UK in comparison with our major economic competitors. However while Luff promotes a greater level of investment from government, Hancock suggests that the solution rests with industry and commerce to make the necessary investment in human capital to respond effectively to the challenge of Europe. Certainly, recent analysis suggests that the current and known levels of skill shortage in the UK will be intensified by an increase in the average skills content of work generated both by the enhanced, and more intensive, commercial competition generated by the Single European Market, and by the greater application of information technology and telecommunications in the workplace (Rajan 1989, 1990).

This situation will be exacerbated by the UK's poor investment record in vocational education, a position which has been visualized by Finegold and Soskice as Britain,

> . . . trapped in a low-skills equilibrium, in which the majority of enterprises staffed by poorly trained managers and workers produce low-quality goods and services. The term 'equilibrium' is used to connote the self-reinforcing network of societal and state institutions which interact to stifle the demand for improvements in skills levels. This set of political-economic institutions . . . include: the organization of industry, firms and the work process, the industrial relations system, financial markets, the state and political structure, as well as the operation of the education and training system. (Finegold and Soskice, 1988, p. 22)

This failure to educate and train the UK work-force at levels equivalent to our international competitors is seen by Finegold and Soskice as both a product and a cause of the UK's relatively poor economic performance, a product because the vocational education system:

> . . . evolved to meet the needs of the world's first industrialized economy, whose large, mass-production manufacturing sector required only a small number of skilled workers and university graduates; and a cause, because the absence of a well-educated and trained work-force has made it difficult for industry to respond to new economic conditions. (1988, p. 21)

This relatively poor comparative performance begins during the years of compulsory education (Prais and Wagner 1983, Lynn 1988) and is reflected in the percentage of young people remaining in full-time education post-16. Indeed in comparison with the UK's major economic competitors, where between 80 and 90 per cent of teenagers are undertaking full-time education or structured apprenticeships, the UK lags significantly behind (OECD 1985, Finegold and Soskice 1988, EDTA 1989). However recent projections from the Department of Employment (DoE 1990) suggests a number of marked changes in the participation of young people in education and employment over the next decade. In particular (all figures relate to Great Britain):

- the number of young people leaving school has fallen steadily from 930,000 in 1980–1 to 790,000 in 1987–8 and is projected to continue falling to 618,000 in 1993–4 before rising over subsequent years to 707,000 in 2000–1;
- estimates for 1987–8 show a staying-on rate at school that is 35 per

cent higher than previously projected among young people reaching middle and school-leaving age. Staying-on rate is projected to continue rising, reaching some 42 per cent in the late 1990s, a figure still significantly below a number of our major economic competitors;

- the proportion of school leavers expected to enter full-time further or higher education is projected to rise from 33 per cent in 1987-8 to some 36 per cent in 1997-8 and subsequently, this trend in part reflecting the higher staying-on rate at school;
- as a consequence of a higher rate of participation in post-compulsory education the number of school leavers available to enter the labour market is projected to show a steep decline from 473,000 in 1989-90 to 402,000 in 1993-4, the 1993-4 figure being some 40 per cent less than the 658,000 young people who entered the labour market in 1982-3;
- among school leavers available to enter the labour market those leaving school at the minimum age are expected to form a smaller proportion in the future years, 72 per cent in 1992-3 compared to 78 per cent in 1986-7.

While encouraging, these trends still suggest that the UK economy has a significantly lower qualificatory base available to it at the point of entry into employment than its major economic competitors. Equally this relatively crude, though significant, indicator may reflect unfavourably both on the initial vocational competence of the work-force, and on the propensity of that work-force to embrace regular retraining and adopt a positive attitude towards self-motivated lifelong learning. Indeed there is little evidence that these trends have been compensated for by the quantity and quality of vocational education provided directly, or indirectly, by employers. While there is a paucity of detailed information about the extent of in-house, employer-led vocational education undertaken in the UK, that which is available suggests:

- it has not been perceived as a major managerial priority (Coopers and Lybrand, 1985);
- it has rarely been integrated into the individual's career structure or reward system (George and Shorey, 1985);
- where continuing training does occur it has been treated for accounting purposes as a variable operating cost and therefore at risk during periods of commercial, or in the public sector funding, downturn (Anderson, 1987).

Combined, these analyses give weight to the views expressed by Luff and Hancock and may, in part, be seen as those behind recent government initiatives such as the Management Charter Initiative, the emerging

Training and Enterprise Councils, and the introduction of training credits for 16-year-old school leavers.

The implications of the Single European Market produce new challenges for vocational education. Importantly however they also emphasize historic weaknesses. These go beyond a relative failure to train, and may be seen as part of a cultural heritage which undervalues vocational educational achievement, and pays scant regard to the relationship between individual capability and competence and economic growth. These issues are considered by Luff and Hancock who conclude that urgent action is required if the UK is not to fall victim to the challenge of the Single European Market.

References

Anderson, A (1987) 'Adult Training: Private Industry and the Nicholson Letter' in A Harrison and J Grettan (eds) *Education and Training UK*, Policy Journals

Cecchini, P (1988) *1992 and the Benefits of a Single Market*, Wildwood House, Aldershot

Coopers and Lybrand Associates (1985) *A Challenge to Complacency: Changing Attitudes to Training*, MSC/NEDO, Moorfoot, Sheffield

Employment Department Training Agency (1989) *Training in Britain: The Main Report*, HMSO, London

Department of Employment (1990) 'Young People Leaving School', *Employment Gazette* vol. 98, no. 8

Finegold, D and Soskice, D (1988) 'The Failure of Training in Britain: Analysis and Prescription', *Oxford Review of Economic Policy*, 4, 3

Further Education Unit (1989) *Towards a Framework for Curriculum Entitlement*, Further Education Unit, DES, London

George, K D and Shorey, J (1985) 'Manual Workers, Good Jobs and Structured Internal Labour Markets', *British Journal of Industrial Relations*, 23, 3

Lynn, R (1988) *Educational Achievement in Japan*, Macmillan, Basingstoke

Müller, D and Funnell, P (1991) *Delivering Quality in Vocational Education*, Kogan Page, London

OECD (1985) *Education and Training After Basic Schooling*, OECD, Paris

Prais, S J and Wagner, K (1983) 'Schooling Standards in Britain and Germany', National Institute of Economic and Social Research, London; discussion paper 60

Rajan, A (1989) *Vocational Training scenario for member states of the European Community: A synthesis and evaluation*, CEDEFOP, Berlin

Rajan, A (1990) *1992: A Zero Sum Game*, Industrial Society Press, London

1 The Single European Market – its Rationale and Consequences

Peter Luff

Reluctant Europeans

The biggest problem facing the British in their relations with the rest of the European Community is that they still think of Europe as being somewhere else. From weather forecasters describing the progression of climatic fronts moving from the British Isles 'into Europe', to managers and tourists speaking of 'going to Europe' for business or pleasure, there lingers deep in the British psyche a profound sense of separation from our continental neighbours. Even quality newspapers will put European Community matters under the heading of foreign news and, at the lower end of the trade, it appears that banner headlines attacking our Community partners, either collectively or individually, using a variety of demeaning nicknames, still sell newspapers.

It is as if, despite our long history of exploration and conquest and the increasing number of tourists who leave our shores every year, we still suffer from what can only be described as a 'fear of foreigners'. It is a fear that has been nurtured by the trauma of war, the extraordinarily rapid loss of an empire and the consequent retreat into insularity. And, of course, the nearest foreigners to be feared live a mere 22 miles away across the thin sleeve of water that divides us from the European continent.

At the best of times, this sense of separateness is unattractive; today, unless there is a radical change of perception, it could begin to spell the end of the economic and political viability of the United Kingdom.

The fact is that we live in Europe. We are Europeans. For all our recorded history, even during the brief period of our 'imperial adventure' when these small islands took centre stage in the theatre of world affairs, our political, economic and military fortunes were intimately interconnected with those of our European neighbours. The wars we fought were essentially European wars fought upon a world scale; our contributions to philosophical, scientific and cultural thought have been within the context of the wider European tradition. Since 1973, when we signed the Treaty of Rome and, perhaps even more importantly, since the referendum of 1975, when the British people voted by a two-to-one margin to remain in the European Community, the majority of our economic and trading life has taken place within Europe. Yet we are still reluctant to think and feel European.

If there were ever times when such insularity made sense, they have certainly disappeared for ever. Our future now depends not just upon knowing the facts about the process of European integration but being able to identify emotionally and intuitively with the greater 'European Idea'.

Jean Monnet, whose unrelenting determination to build a united Europe earned him the title of 'the Founding Father of Europe', once said of the British, 'There is one thing you British will never understand: an idea. And there is one thing you are supremely good at grasping: a hard fact. We will have to build Europe without you, but you will then come and join us.' These words have been prophetically true, and to our continental partners, they are becoming a trifle wearying. The post-war generation of European statesmen who drafted the Treaties of Paris and Rome, the Stuttgart Declaration and the Single European Act, were not primarily motivated by the need to harmonize 'plugs and sockets' but by a vision of a European union or, more colloquially, a United States of Europe, that would defy history and preserve, through its unique institutions, perpetual peace and economic progress in Europe.

Monnet also said, and this is perhaps the key to the change that must take place in Britain if we are to play our full part, that if he were to begin the construction of Europe again, he would start with education. It was an acutely perceptive statement from a man who had been involved with virtually all the different political, economic and social threads which were being drawn into the extraordinarily complex tapestry of European Community relations. At the very heart of the notion of European union lies the need for people to understand and accept the process of European integration and to have the necessary mental and physical resources to enable them to adapt their ambitions, ideas and life-styles to the new structures that will arise.

For most people, this can only happen effectively through a combination of education and training: education that will open minds to the broader concepts of European political and social change; and training that will provide relevant skills and knowledge to enable people to succeed in the new economic conditions that will be created not only by the process of European integration but also by the unparalleled contemporary revolutions in science and technology.

Indeed, the construction of the European Community and scientific

21

progress particularly in the field of information technology and telecommunications have been inextricably interlinked. The development of a Single European Market would have been practically inconceivable were it not for the sophistication of modern technology. Although there is a growing understanding of the complex relationship between European integration and the technological revolution, it has not yet been sufficiently incorporated into the conceptual frameworks of our educational system. At all levels of society, from senior management to public transport, from financial services to corner shops, from teaching to sport, our lives are being transformed not just by technology and by European integration but also by their interplay. It is not legislation that will bring Europe together, but the experience of new languages coming through the switchboard and on the computer screen, new systems and structures sweeping aside older and less productive methods, new styles of thought and practice competing with the familiar.

The importance of education and training

If we are to survive and prosper, more and more will depend upon our ability to educate, train and retrain not just our young people but the wider workforce. Indeed, education and training have become the cornerstones of all successful modern economies. In this respect, we have much to learn from our European partners who have shown a far greater preparedness to make education and training a priority for national investment. Britain, on the other hand, has failed to recognize the critical importance of a highly skilled and qualified work-force in today's economic climate and is now having to face the problems that a lack of investment during the past decade is bringing to light. The gap between those young people who have obtained higher academic, vocational or professional qualifications, and those who have not, is forecast to grow considerably in the Single European Market, which will put a high premium on skilled labour. Although there are different approaches and attitudes to the acquisition of expertise – continental employers expect their graduates to be fully professionally trained whereas British and Irish employers expect to provide further training on the job – for those who leave school with nothing but the bare minimum, the future may look increasingly bleak.

In addition to all these factors, demographic changes are going to play a key role in structuring employment opportunities over the next two decades. The sharp decline in the number of young people who will be seeking work during this period is already giving forecasters and planners severe worries. With fewer young people available, the job market will offer far greater opportunities to women returning to the work-force after child-bearing, to part-time and job-sharing workers, and to older people prepared to undertake retraining. In all cases, success will depend upon the adaptability of our educational and training services and the resources which they are given by government.

Broadening the sectors of society from which the work-force will be drawn will also have the effect of strengthening the social aspects of European legislation to protect both basic rights and fair competition. Again, technology and telecommunications will increasingly set the parameters within which training methods and standards can be measured across the continent.

We also have to face the increasing problem of the lack of language skills in this country. Still at the bottom of the European league table for the ability to speak a second Community language, it is disheartening to find that, whereas the number of 'A' level pupils has steadily increased over the past decade, the number of pupils studying a foreign language has declined both in absolute numbers and in relation to other subjects studied. However committed we may be to the free movement of people within an open market for skills, no legislation can overcome a failure to communicate in other languages. Indeed, language is one barrier that may well be raised as the others come down for those who speak two or more Community languages will always be free to sell in their competitors' languages but buy in their own.

Although a vast amount still needs to be done, there has been an awakening during the past three years to the critical importance of the relationship between European awareness, educational qualifications, training needs and languages, not just by business and training providers but also in schools, colleges and universities. Indeed the change in attitude since the end of 1988, when the Department of Trade and Industry (DTI) awareness campaign began to bite, has been quite remarkable.

Whereas at one stage 1992 and the single market programme seemed to be the British Government's best-kept secret, today educational institutions and training providers are fighting to get the resources necessary to incorporate a European dimension into the curriculum. Tragically, the resources are still lacking to generate the revolution in attitudes required to bridge the gap in awareness and information about Europe that divides us from most, if not all, of our continental neighbours.

Promoting change: national and European initiatives

It is, of course, dangerous to generalize too glibly about the difference in European awareness between British and continental students. There exists very little hard information, except in relation to language-learning where the disparity is great, but the experience of exchange programmes and the testimony of individual teachers and business people indicates overwhelmingly that young people in most other EC member states are far more aware of the importance of the European dimension to both their careers and their civic lives than are their British contemporaries.

Much is being done to change this in the voluntary sector. Organizations such as the UK Committee for European Education and the European Movement organize European awareness conferences for as many as resources allow. The Central Bureau for Educational Visits and Exchanges has major exchange programmes for pupils and other young people. The Centre for Information on Language Teaching (CILT) continues to provide both information and training on language-learning while campaigning for an increased commitment to it in the UK. European Work Exchange, as the name implies, finds placements for young people in Britain and the continent which will enable them to gain work-place experience in another Community country.

As well as national initiatives, the European Community itself has developed a number of educational and training programmes designed to turn the concept of free movement of people into reality. It has always been appreciated that without offering opportunities for exchange and travel and the chance to experience life in other member states the removal of the internal barriers would mean very little to many young people. The Community has concentrated, therefore, on schemes that place education and training within the context of intra-community travel.

Although European exchange programmes have been in operation for many years, the European Community Action Scheme for the Mobility of University Students (ERASMUS) has added a new dimension. By covering tuition fees and helping with grants to cover additional expenses, the scheme is designed to encourage students to spend part of their courses at a university in another Community country. Aimed at all subject areas and with a component that allows teaching staff to spend at least a month at a higher education establishment in another member state, the ERASMUS programme is also attempting to make the point that language-learning is not just for linguists but for those studying each and every subject at university level.

The Community Programme in Education and Training for Technology (COMETT) is similarly constituted to encourage trans-national training schemes for those involved in post-secondary scientific and technological education but it goes further by initiating placements for students in companies in other member states and setting up cross-border exchanges between universities and industrial personnel. Both are schemes designed to encourage a familiarity with the culture, language and working practices of other Community countries.

The LINGUA programme, whose implementation in Britain the British Government tried unsuccessfully to oppose, was set up to encourage language-learning throughout the Community by developing the initial training of foreign language teachers, promoting in-service training courses for language teachers wishing to develop their linguistic skills further and encouraging exchanges for young people undergoing professional, vocational and technical education. If LINGUA is primarily for teachers, the EURYDICE and ARION programmes foster exchanges between educational authority personnel in order to improve mutual knowledge and understanding of member states' differing education systems, and to collect and disseminate information on Community and member state action in the field of education, training and youth.

Set up in 1987 for a five-year period, the Community Action Programme for the Vocational Training of Young People and their Preparation for Adult Working Life (PETRA) assists young people who wish to receive one year's, or if possible two or more years' vocational training upon completion of their compulsory education. It also aims to diversify training so as to make it suitable for all young people and ensure that it leads to recognized qualifications, and to enhance the capacity of training systems for economic, social and technological change within a European framework.

Other Community schemes include EuroTecnet, which is developing vocational training in the new technologies; IRIS, a Community network of training programmes for women; and CEDEFOP, a Community body whose task is to promote the development of vocational training at Community level. This series of acronyms, seemingly sufficient to repel even the most fanatical Europhile, have, in fact, attracted as much, if not more, attention from British educational institutions as from any other member state. Possibly because of the lack of resources available at home, the Commission has been overwhelmed by applications from the United Kingdom. That this should continue is important, not least because it will encourage those responsible to press for greater financial resources to be given to these key programmes.

Business has also responded, both individually and collectively, to the need to support training and educational initiatives geared to the European dimension. The Employment Department Training Agency has piloted training access points (TAPs) which offer local and national information on training opportunities for the single market. The Department of Education and Science adapted the Professional, Industrial and Commercial Updating Programme (PICKUP) to help colleges, polytechnics and universities provide more and improved vocational courses for employers who wish to retrain or update the skills of their work-force. Local Employer Networks, based on local chambers of commerce, will provide advice on the effect 1992 will have upon local labour market trends and training needs. Additionally, the CBI and the DTI have developed computer-based information and retrieval services for companies seeking a path through the maze, and most professional bodies have begun intensive programmes of training and information provision for their members.

It all looks very impressive, but the reality is that we still have a very long way to go if our vocational education provisions are to meet our needs.

One of the main problems still to be faced is that British schools' curricula, despite the recent plethora of changes, including the introduction of a national curriculum, still pay scant attention to the needs of the European market. Unlike a growing number of other European states' systems, there is no provision for language-learning at the primary level and a considerable lack of language teaching resources at secondary level. Little attention is paid to the historical, political and economic issues raised by our membership of the European Community and the degree of specialization at 'A' level, though less than previously, is still far greater than on the continent. One solution to this problem has been the growing number of schools and colleges attracted to the International Baccalaureate which, in common with most European systems, allows for at least six subjects to be taken up to the age of eighteen.

We are moving at speed into a new environment in which people will be free to use their skills and talents both in cooperation and competition with others in eleven other countries. The implications are extraordinary and exciting: it is not too difficult to imagine the scenario recently described in the newspaper *The European*:

> Enter the new Euro-citizens, a couple dazzled by choice. They are buying their home in Italy with a Dutch mortgage. He works for a Danish company; she is a partner in a Greek firm of architects. They insure their family car in Germany and he buys his shirts from a French mail order company and she her dresses from Brussels. Their daughter studied in Paris and Edinburgh and now works in Luxembourg. Their son is a Euro-apprentice with VW in Spain.

Naturally, this scenario will only apply in its totality to a small proportion of the citizens of any Community country. The question we must ask, however, is if we find ourselves living in a Europe as integrated as the article suggests, how will the British fare and what can be done through education and training to improve their chances? If people generally, and young people in particular, are to make sense of the new European environment in which they will be pursuing their careers, they urgently need both factual information and an awareness of the political and economic principles governing the dynamics of integration. Yet the underlying trends and currents of contemporary European thought are rarely taught or discussed in anything but a cursory way. If, when 1992 arrives, the concept of Europe still remains a vague and undefined notion for the British, the time for change may well have past.

Towards European unity

The successful development of the European Community can largely be attributed to an early appreciation of the need to let its institutions grow *sui generis* rather than tying them to a fixed constitution as in the USA. This fluidity of approach enabled the sometimes contradictory demands of national and Community objectives to be reconciled while steadily moving forward the process of unification. If most of the institutions were, self-evidently, political, they grew out of a need to make the increasing number of supranational economic decisions democratically accountable to the people of Europe, either directly or through their national parliaments. But the underlying imperative has always been the need to achieve full European economic, monetary and political union.

Those in Britain who doubt this should read the reports of the two Congresses of Europe held in the Hague in 1948 and on the fortieth anniversary of the original Congress, in 1988, at which statesmen and women of both the post-war generation and modern Europe set out their visions of the future. Many, like François Mitterrand and Richard von Weiszecker, who had listened intently in 1948, when the Congress was chaired by Sir Winston Churchill, spoke in 1988 with the authority of their positions as European prime ministers and heads of state. Yet they retained the same sense of urgency and conviction about European union that imbued the original Congress two generations previously. For Britain to fail to comprehend the strength of this political tide, especially since the dramatic changes in the Soviet Union and Eastern Europe have so completely altered the framework of reference in which the world was understood, is no longer eccentric but positively dangerous to our political and economic interests.

While the old structures of Europe have changed almost beyond imagining, the outline of the new architecture is only just beginning to appear. There is, however, one fixed point which is perceived by European nations, both East and West, as the key to future stability: the European Community. As the possibility of widening the membership of the Community becomes desirable and possible, the need to deepen political, monetary and economic relations between the present twelve members of the Community becomes ever more urgent. One process depends upon the other: if the newly democratic states of Central and Eastern Europe, the European Free Trade Association countries, and possibly Turkey, should wish to join the European Community it would be preposterous to expect the existing institutions to cope with two dozen or more sovereign states each arguing, with the power of veto, for their national interests. Deepening and widening the relationships both within the Community and between the twelve and other European nations are two sides of the same coin.

A third aspect relates to the first two – reforming the institutions of the Community in order to make them more efficient, accountable and democratic and to prevent any one member state from having an economic or political strength sufficient to frustrate the collective will of the other members. The Community's institutions have evolved out of dynamic interaction between economic integration and political control. Usually, though not always, economic integration has outstripped the democratic decision-making process and this has never been more noticeable than at present.

With the single market well on its way to completion and the first steps being taken towards monetary union, there now exists a real danger that the expression of the will of the people of Europe is being frustrated by what is sometimes called the 'democratic deficit'. This recognizes that while an increasing number of key decisions are being made by Community institutions, neither the Council of Ministers or the European Commission is directly elected by, or accountable to, the people of Europe.

It was to meet these issues head on that two parallel intergovernmental conferences, on monetary and political union, were convened in the winter of 1990. While it is too early fully to assess the significance of these events, it is certain that they will hasten progress towards full European union. For if there is one point upon which both those who favour and those who oppose monetary union are agreed, it is that it will, to all intents and purposes, mean political union but without democratic control.

Where the two camps then divide is that the former believes the solution is to increase the powers of the key democratic arm of the Community – the European Parliament – while the latter believes it is necessary and possible to return to greater national sovereignty over key decisions even if this leads to isolation within the Community. But isolation is something Britain can no longer afford, as we realized when we signed the Treaty of Rome and, more recently, the Single European Act. By ratifying the Single European Act, we accepted the objective of the 1992 programme which was to weld the economic and trading potential of twelve separate states into one single market.

The 'cost of 'non-Europe' and the Single European Market

As with all the treaties binding the European Community, the Single European Act, which provides the enabling legislation for the 1992 programme, is a mixture of political, economic, social and environmental issues. Its name derives from the bringing together of a number of diverse topics into a single treaty and not, as is supposed by many people, from the concept of a single Europe. Although it was a new treaty, which needed to be ratified by the parliaments of the twelve member states, its effect was to amend the Treaty of Rome and strengthen some of its provisions, particularly those relating to the free movement of goods, people, capital and services.

The first step towards developing the European Economic Community (now more commonly called the European Community or EC) was taken in 1950 when the French Foreign Minister, Robert Schuman, proposed the creation of a European Coal and Steel Community (ECSC) to establish a common basis for economic development and as a first step towards the federation of Europe. This bold idea, which would bring the production and consumption of the two key heavy industries of north-west Europe under the authority of a supranational high authority, proved acceptable to six states – France, The Federal Republic of Germany, Italy, Belgium, The Netherlands and Luxembourg – and the Treaty of Paris, which created the ECSC, was signed in April 1951.

The success of the ECSC encouraged the six to prepare plans for further economic integration and, at Messina in 1955, the foreign ministers asked Paul Henri Spaak, the Belgian Minister, to prepare a report on the complete merger of the six economies and a plan for the pooling of resources in the development of nuclear energy. The result was two new treaties, the first setting up the European Atomic Energy Community (Euratom) and the second – the Treaty of Rome – establishing the European Economic Community, which was signed in March 1957.

At each stage of these developments, the British Government was warmly invited to participate by the governments of the six but to their considerable disappointment, Britain chose instead to create a far looser grouping of European States – the European Free Trade Association (EFTA). Within a decade, however, it became clear that the growth in the economies of the six, who were reaping the benefits of a common market free of tariff barriers, far outstripped that of the UK, who tried twice, unsuccessfully, to join the Community in the mid-sixties.

It was not until 1973 that the United Kingdom, the Republic of Ireland and Denmark signed the Treaty of Rome and took their places as full members of the European Community. Two years later, following a change of government in Britain, a referendum was held in which the British people voted by a margin of two-to-one to stay in the Community. The Community grew again in the early nineteen eighties with the accession of Greece in 1981 and Spain and Portugal in 1986. By the mid-1980s, however, there was a growing awareness that the initial impetus had begun to slow down, especially in respect to the other two major trading groups in the world: the United States and Canada, and Japan and the newly industrialized nations of the Pacific rim.

In most areas of the economy, but most especially in the key sector of high technology exports, the EC was falling behind. Indeed by the mid-1980s it was clear that in the exportation of high technology goods as a percentage of all manufactured goods the United States had increased its lead, while Japan had overtaken the EC. One result of the Community's sluggish economic performance, which had never fully recovered from the energy crisis of the mid-1970s, could be seen vividly in the steadily rising level of unemployment, most especially among the young and ill-trained. Once again, the political analysis of those who desired to see a more united Europe coincided with the need to generate economic growth in the Community. The solution was to find ways of removing the remaining economic barriers to free trade and industrial and commercial cooperation. That the remaining barriers to trade were hampering growth was self-evident but their clear identification and articulation required a formidable programme of research.

The Cecchini Report (Cecchini, 1988), which distilled information provided by over 11,000 business people throughout the EC, demonstrated the heavy costs of having twelve different markets divided by frontier controls and other less tangible barriers. The report went on to estimate the financial benefits that could accrue from the creation of a single market. Although some of the report's claims have been disputed in subsequent research, it remains the most comprehensive and detailed analysis of the 'cost of non-Europe', the term used to describe the financial burdens caused by a fragmented market. A number of key problems facing European business were identified and, of these, four were of particular importance.

The most obstructive barriers to cross-border trade, in the view of most business people, were the administrative formalities and the border controls to which they are so often linked. Paper work and frontier-checks, lorries queuing to get through customs posts and the frustrations of the immigration controls were not just irritations for the traveller; their cost to business could be measured in billions of European Currency Units (ECUs). In 1987, EC-wide firms paid around Ecu 8 billion in administrative costs and delays, occasioned by intra-EC customs procedures – a sum equivalent to some 2 per cent of the value of these trans-border sales. The delays also occasioned a loss of turnover amounting to somewhere between Ecu 5 and 15 billion. In addition were the costs to governments, or rather their tax-payers, of providing the human resources necessary to maintain the controls, estimated at between Ecu 500–1,000 million – all figures at 1987 prices (Cecchini, 1988).

A second, more hidden cost, was caused by government protectionism in the area of public procurement. Although cross-border tendering was acceptable for certain products, the largest areas of procurement, in particular telecommunications, energy, transport and water, were subject to a high degree of protectionism. The Cecchini Report concluded that massive savings could result from allowing public authorities to buy from the cheapest sources available without the constraint of governmental protectionist practice. Increased competition and the restructuring effect of industries could have a downward effect upon prices and industry would not only be allowed to increase specialization but also be forced into greater innovation, investment and growth. Savings in this area were estimated at around Ecu 17.5 billion or around 0.5 per cent of 1986 Community Gross Domestic Product.

Thirdly, and possibly the greatest handicap to Community growth, were the divergences in technical regulations and standards. The need to produce different products for each of the twelve national markets effectively prevented any advantages deriving from economies of scale. Here there were an infinite number of examples, from high-tech goods such as computers to the most lowly of household goods and services. It was not just the differing standards that handicapped cross-border trade but the willingness of Community governments to use technical regulations as another form of protectionism that defeated the objectives set out in the Treaty of Rome.

Finally, and most crucially for the extraordinary amount of intellectual talent that abounded in the twelve nations of the Community, enormous resources were being wasted on duplicating research and development initiatives. In particular, language barriers led to the dissipation of investment that could have yielded far greater results if there had been a unified approach to research in Europe. Both the US and Japan achieved more cost-effective results for a smaller financial outlay.

These were some of the key problems that the Community set out to tackle through the Single European Act and the Single European Market programme. The Single European Act incorporated seven major areas of Community policy related to the creation of a unified market:

- reform of the legislative procedures of the European Parliament and the Council of Ministers in order to speed up the passage of single market legislation;

- the removal of the remaining non-tariff barriers to trade, with 31 December 1992 set as the date for completion;
- a commitment to further cooperation in economic and monetary policies;
- the development of a social dimension of the Community in order to promote social 'cohesion';
- the strengthening of research and technological development policies;
- the recognition that environmental concerns should play a major role in all aspects of Community legislation;
- greater European cooperation in the sphere of foreign policy and a commitment to progress towards political union.

It can be seen much more clearly now than was generally recognized by the British Parliament when it ratified the Act in 1986, that all the parts of the Act are interconnected, complementary and enjoy political and popular support through much of Europe. There had been a tendency in UK political circles to assume that the only materially significant part of the Act related to the removal of the barriers to trade. Although the 1992 programme was the most immediately dynamic feature of the legislation, it became clear that the Commission and other member governments intended to pursue the other provisions of the Act with almost equal energy. This can be seen in the production of a Social Charter, the Delors plan on monetary union, the inter-governmental conferences on monetary and political union during 1990 and the establishment of an environmental agency.

Implementing the Single European Act

Two key institutional changes were introduced by the Single European Act. The first was the adoption of a system of qualified majority-voting in the Council of Ministers for most of the 1992 programme. The second was a right of amendment by the European Parliament upon the second reading of proposed legislation. Such amendments could only be subsequently rejected, if supported by the Commission, by a unanimous vote in the Council of Ministers. The system of qualified majority-voting, which gave the largest countries 12 votes and then a declining number down to Luxembourg with two votes, required a majority of 54 out of 76 votes for legislation to be approved. The effect of this has been to speed up dramatically the Community's legislative process to the point when it had an odds-on chance of completing the programme by 1992.

A further important factor which underlay the development of the single market came not directly from the legislators but from the interpreters of Community law – The European Court. Moving away from the need for complete harmonization of standards before goods could travel automatically between member states, the Court struck a blow for the wider concept of 'mutual recognition'. In delivering a judgement in favour of the French who were objecting to the refusal of the Federal Republic of Germany to allow the importation of a French liqueur, Cassis de Dijon, which contravened ancient German liquor laws, the Court insisted that, with key exceptions, it was against the principles of free trade to restrict importation of such a product unless refusal was based upon reasons of health, safety or consumer protection. The European Court found in the case of Cassis de Dijon that, as none of these conditions applied, it was illegal to prevent the product from being sold in another member state. The Court left the matter of its acceptability as a beverage to the discriminating taste of the German consumer. A key exception to this principle concerned cross-border trading in financial services, where the viability of the company as well as the product would have to be guaranteed in order to protect the consumer.

Although this ruling was to help considerably the progress towards a single market, the need to find common standards relating to all aspects of health, safety and consumer protection still left the European Commission with an enormous task. This task was undertaken by a team under the direction of Lord Cockfield, a British-appointed Vice President of the European Community, and resulted in a white paper that incorporated the proposed legislation to create a single market in the form of 300 directives. This has since been reduced by amalgamation to 282.

Directives are forms of Community legislation which are binding on all member states in respect of the results to be achieved and the time period for achievement, but leave the method of implementation to national governments. These differ significantly from other forms of legislation, namely: regulations, which are directly binding on all member states without flexibility of implementation; decisions, which are only binding on those to whom they are addressed; and recommendations and opinions, which have no binding force.

The directives to complete the single market were broken down into three, now familiar, categories:

- physical barriers – in other words, border controls including immigration and customs and excise;
- fiscal barriers, which involved finding a solution to problems caused by widely varying VAT levies and excise duties;
- technical barriers, the politically least contentious but technically most complex area of harmonization.

The technical barriers, which comprise the large majority of the directives, will have both the most immediate and long-term effect upon educational and training initiatives throughout the Community. In essence, they have implications for virtually every business and profession in the Community. From building regulations to food additives, from banking regulations to fuel emission, they will affect all sectors of industry and commerce and by extension, the whole work-force.

Knowledge of Community proposals will be essential for all those seeking professional and vocational qualifications. Almost any field of work may be used as an example:

- insurance agents will need to be aware of the Non-Life Insurance Services directive and its implementation both in the UK and other member states;
- transport companies will need to be familiar with regulations concerning the freedom to provide services and unfair pricing practices, as well as many other relevant Community laws;
- grocers will already be very aware of the numerous directives concerning additives, labelling and food composition.

The list is enormous and will cover almost all aspects of commercial life. Yet, despite the importance of the information being widely disseminated throughout all levels of industry, the likelihood of it reaching any but a handf il of senior executive staff in most companies remains remote. What is needed, both as we approach and pass the 1992 deadline, is a massive investment programme aimed at stimulating awareness among the existing work-force. However such a development is extremely unlikely in the near future. More optimistically, the fact that some colleges have already incorporated a European dimension into the curriculum of most vocational and professional courses will mean that a more aware and better informed working population will soon be entering employment.

The most direct effect upon vocational and professional training and qualifications will come from the General Directive which provides for the mutual recognition throughout the Community of all professional qualifications that require three years education at university level or its equivalent. The aim is to implement this General Directive by January 1991, at which time all professionals whose qualifications fall within its scope will have the right to have their qualifications recognized in another member state. Quite clearly, in some cases there will be substantial differences in both the type of training and the information required to practice a profession in another member state. In such cases, those who have the recognized qualification will have the choice between either an aptitude test, designed to assess their ability to pursue their profession in the host member state, or a period of supervised practice not exceeding three years.

By mid-1990, over half the measures required to create the single market had been adopted by the Council of Ministers. These needed only to be incorporated into national legislations – a process that varies considerably in speed throughout the Community. Highly centralized states, such as the United Kingdom, generally achieve much faster incorporation than federally structured states like West Germany. Most of the measures will have been discussed by the two relevant committees: Comité Européen de Normalisation (CEN) or Comité de Normalisation Electro-technique (CENELEC) upon which representatives from relevant trade associations and national standards committees fight to uphold their national and commercial interests.

Most of the remaining proposals have been drafted by the Commission but still need the approval of the Parliament and the Council of Ministers. Of the remaining legislation, 20 per cent concerns the politically contentious areas of border control and tax harmonization which still require unanimity in the Council.

In addition to removing barriers to internal trade, the Commission has paid considerable attention to the importance of creating a 'level playing field' upon which member states, regions and localities can compete with as great a degree of fairness as possible. The Community's structural funds have been used to ensure that social contrasts are not so great as to distort competition by providing matching resources for training and infrastructural spending. The United Kingdom has benefited, and continues to benefit, from this spending and projects as diverse as Birmingham's National Exhibition Centre, and small-scale industrial and vocational training schemes have received support from the Community's Social Fund.

The social dimension

The social dimension of the Single European Act has been incorporated into a Social Charter outlining a number of specific social objectives relating to rights, pay and opportunities. Underpinning all industrial and social policies is a commitment to environmental protection backed up by an environmental agency. If, as is becoming apparent, most aspects of our economic, social and environmental life will be affected by the European dimension, the importance to all aspects of vocational and professional training will be obvious. Not least, it will be increasingly important for all those looking to a career in manufacturing or service industry activity to keep abreast of the increasingly stringent rules the Community is laying down for environmental protection and the obligations which will be set out in the Social Charter.

Employment creation has always been one of the central objectives of the European Community. The Cecchini Report suggested that the economic benefits of the single market programme could be a boost to European Gross Domestic Product of between 5 per cent and 7 per cent, with the creation of up to five million new jobs. If this estimate looked unduly hopeful when it was first published, employment and unemployment trends in the Community for the period 1985 to 1989 seem to confirm the report's optimism. In those four years, employment in the Community increased by seven million, a sustained rate of employment growth unsurpassed since the 1950s. It was forecast to increase still further by one-and-a-half million in 1990 and a million in 1991.

At the same time that employment rose, unemployment fell until it stood, at the end of 1989, at 12.5 million – 8.5 per cent of the Community's working population. Again, the decline is predicted to continue. These figures bear further analysis. Of the five million jobs created between 1985–89, nearly three million were filled by women. Although the rate of increase in female employment was, in most member states, roughly double that of the increase in male employment, the number of women out of work actually rose by almost 350,000. The reason for this was the large number of jobs that went to young people coming on to the labour market for the first time or people who, up until finding a job, had not been counted as unemployed. The majority of these new entrants into the labour market were women. Forty per cent of the new jobs were part-time. The majority of the jobs created were in the service sector and related activities and within this sector, the highest growth took place in health, education and other social sectors, which alone accounted for over two million jobs.

Prospects for the 1990s

Prospects for the 1990s look even brighter. Although much remains to be done, particularly in the UK, there has been a significant reaction by many large companies to the prospect of the single market. The DTI campaign, which initially alerted British business to the opportunities and threats of the market, seems to have penetrated through to the overwhelming majority of British businesses. According to the CBI, over 93 per cent of British companies claim to have, at least, some awareness of the 1992 programme. A significant number have taken the first steps towards examining the implications for their business. Quite clearly, the implications will vary enormously between those international corporations who will have begun the re-thinking and restructuring processes long before the campaign began and those small and medium-sized enterprises who will be taking their first uncertain steps towards an evaluation of the possibilities of international trade.

Most companies, of course, will fall in the middle and will be looking to the results of any audit or revaluation of product, management and marketing needs before taking further steps. A surprising number, however, have already begun to make enquiries about merger with compatible companies in other Community countries. By the beginning of 1990, the European Commission reported a quadrupled increase in merger activities in the last five years over the previous five. It also identified the industrial sectors which stand to be most affected by the 1992 measures and the changes most likely to take place.

In the first instance, the most immediate effect on job-seekers will be felt by those with higher and further education, and/or professional qualifications. A recent report on Corporate Employment Policies for the Single European Market (Atkinson, 1989) identified corporate demand for international mobility and recruitment of labour as being largely restricted to four groups of employee: the most senior managers; younger managers on a development programme to place them in this senior group; leading scientific and technical staff; and, to a lesser extent, graduate recruits. A factor identifying the potential demand for international mobility was a corporate concern about skill shortages (current and prospective, and numerical and qualitative). These will have the effect of increasing the number of employees from whom such mobility is sought, as firms cast a wider recruitment net and/or relocate existing staff to fill vacant posts.

As the political and economic influence of the Community grows, however, the effect will not just be felt by those who see mobility as part of their career prospects but also increasingly by those working in their country of origin who find an increasing international dimension to their work. An Oxfordshire-based tertiary college recently telephoned two dozen firms in the Thames Valley area and tried to make themselves understood in French and German. In only two cases were they able to get beyond the switchboard. As more and more firms combine across national borders in order to expand their interests and protect their markets, a new thinking process will need to be developed not just in the boardroom but right along the executive corridors to the production line. This new thinking will see our fellow Europeans not as 'foreigners' but as genuine partners with whom we can share existing ideas and develop new ones.

It is no exaggeration to say that Britain's economic survival will depend not upon last-ditch struggles to save vestiges of sovereignty but on a determination to invest in the most crucial of resources – the British people – and to enable them to have the education and training necessary to prosper in the new Europe that is being built.

References

Atkinson, J (1989) *Corporate Employment Policies for the Single European Market*, Institute of Manpower Studies, University of Sussex

Cecchini, P. (1988) *1992 and the Benefits of a Single European Market*, Wildwood House, Aldershot

2 The Single European Market – Uncertain Implications and the Vocational Educational Challenge

Colin Hancock

Predicting the implications of the Single European Market

No brave new world will be created on 1 January 1993. The single market will not be finished. It would be possible to go into detail on the predictions contained in the Cecchini Report (Cecchini, 1988) but this would have been of marginal value even before the developments in Eastern Europe during 1989 as no one has yet been able to build a dynamic model of the European economy. Hardly surprising in that, in many areas, statistics are either non-existent or incomplete. We are actually guessing at the economic effects, not knowing the timescale within which they take effect. PROGNOS, the Basle forecasting organization, has predicted that there will be an average annual growth of 2.6 per cent in European Community Gross Domestic Product between 1990 and the end of the century. However it will be in the next century before major beneficial effects of the Single European Market are felt.

Whether or not this growth is realized will depend on industry and commerce. All the evidence relating to capital and inward investment would indicate that there will be a positive effect for the UK but an uneven one. Some predict that the major benefits will flow to the less developed and disadvantaged areas and/or accrue to multi-national corporations. I do not believe this to be entirely the case. Multi-nationals will benefit; however it will be a long time before the infrastructure, services, government efficiency and public service probity in southern Europe matches that of the north. So, these countries will be compensated in the short- to medium-term by increased transfers from enlarged European Community structural funds.

As far as the effects on the EC of recent changes in Eastern Europe are concerned, the situation is still too uncertain to make a firm prediction. However it would appear that although diversion of investment funds, together with higher interest rates, could have some depressant effects on economic activity, this will be more than counter-balanced over the medium term by demand from the East, particularly for investment and capital goods. This has the potential of leading to an overall increase in the growth of EC Gross Domestic Product of some 0.5 per cent. If accurate, this could amount to an annual growth within the EC of over 3 per cent; whether this will be economically sustainable in the UK over the 1990s must be an open question.

Just as for the Community as a whole, whether any particular region of the UK benefits from the Single European Market will initially depend on individual businesses. It is easy to think of excuses for not meeting the challenge – high interest rates, the impact of the unified business rate and so on. But this does not really excuse the long-term decline in Britain's technological competitiveness, which first became evident at the Paris Great Exhibition in the 1860s, nor the overall reluctance to train employees, nor the UK's poor record of investment in new plants and machinery on a coherent basis. Perhaps this is all symptomatic of the reluctance to plan ahead, a reluctance which will leave many firms seriously, even disastrously unprepared for the Single European Market.

Fortunately, overseas companies seem attracted to establishing themselves in the UK, the first choice of both the USA and Japan, with major inward investment being directed to a number of relatively depressed areas in Britain. However this holds its own dangers, for inward investment combined with any general economic upturn will surely ensure, unless positive action is taken, that the UK will once again be faced with the situation where growth is restricted, perhaps even throttled, by labour and skill shortages, with imports pouring in to fill the gap.

The social effect of the Single European Market

This logically brings the discussion to a consideration of the social effect of the Single European Market. Once again there is an absence of comprehensive statistics in this area on a Community-wide basis on which to make firm predictions. It is however possible to consider known demographic factors and the current relative demand for graduates and skilled workers, to identify sectors where a high rate of growth can be anticipated, and then extrapolate. All EC countries except Eire face a fall in the number of young people entering the work-force, and, between now and the year 2010, it is predicted that the total population of Western

Europe will grow only by some 2 per cent. During 1990 some 120,000 graduates will emerge in the UK but: the pool of high calibre graduates remains relatively small; more and more graduates are shunning teaching as a career; the numbers studying engineering are plateauing or declining despite their scarcity value; there are insufficient graduates in a number of fields including 'sunrise industries' such as computer science and electronics.

In many areas of skilled labour the UK is uncompetitive compared with our German, French, South Korean and Japanese competitors. About 90 per cent of 16- and 17-year-olds in Japan and the USA are in full-time education; in the UK the figure for 17-year-olds is some 30 per cent. In Germany technicians hired after they finish their compulsory external training courses attend a technicians school in mid-career and acquire advanced skills. France and South Korea have set ambitious vocational training targets for the year 2000. The UK is only now waking up to the realization that it has a problem. All this is particularly serious in that it is possible to identify certain specific current and predictable future shortage areas which demand high skills levels: electronics, including high definition television; computers; telecommunications and information technology; engineering; and personal communications.

It is quite clear that there will be a prime need to communicate within the Single European Market putting a premium on those with language skills and those able to teach them. Accountancy is an interesting area; while not yet a shortage area it is absorbing more and more graduates in the UK into the process of working out a more efficient distribution of the existing cake rather than enlarging its size. Approximately 11 per cent of graduates entered this area in 1989 and this percentage is predicted to increase further.

Above all the key field of the 1990s and beyond will be electronics which will be involved, to a greater or lesser degree, in 80 per cent of activity. There will not be enough young people to meet the demand. Vocational training and retraining will be vital if skills gaps are to be closed and consequently it would be unwise to neglect any potential re-entrants into the labour market. In this context it is important to acknowledge that women are still in the minority in engineering and computer sciences. As previous attempts to attract women entrants have failed it may be time to consider new approaches both promotional and educational.

Freedom of movement

Discussion of the implications of freedom of movement, like Gaul, divides neatly into three parts: what is the existing law; what changes will occur as a result of the Single European Market; what effect will free movement have?

The present situation, except with regard to Spain and Portugal who will fall in line after 1992, is as follows:

- workers are free to take up or seek work anywhere in the EC;
- workers should be allowed free entry;
- workers cannot be refused a residence permit except on the grounds of public order;
- workers may be subject to medical examination but only within the limits set by Directive 221 of 1964;
- a three-month residence limit exists for unemployed workers;
- individuals should not experience discrimination on grounds of nationality;
- workers and their families are covered by the Social Security provisions of the country of employment.

The changes after 1992 will involve:

- the extension of all rights to the whole family unit;
- the protection of the spouse of a non-Community citizen in the event of death or divorce;
- access of members of the whole family unit to general educational provision, apprenticeships, vocational training and higher education on the same basis as nationals;
- the replacement of national residents permits by an EC resident's card valid for five years, provided that the employment contract held by the individual is for longer than one year.

There will also be a general right of residence for the retired and students, subject to certain social security provisions ensuring that those crossing frontiers do not become a charge on a state in which they have never paid contributions. This will mean that:

- an employer will be able to recruit anywhere in the European Community and any EC citizen may apply;
- a major difficulty for any employer will be in judging the equivalent levels of qualifications of potential applicants.

Given mutual recognition between member states there should be no problem with regard to those holding professional qualifications and diplomas. However the Commission may have underestimated the problem associated with the widely differing standards prevailing across the Community in relation to diplomas and other qualifications awarded after a course of less than three years. This is an area currently the subject of a draft proposal from the Commission.

The real area of difficulty however lies with vocational qualifications. Work in designing equivalents is proceeding, and we have already seen tables published in the *Official Journal of the European Communities (OJEC)* concerning workers in motor vehicle repair, construction and hotel and catering among others. In retailing an agreement has been reached on what courses should earn a European Vocational Training Card, though it should be noted that this was as a result of an agreement between management and unions in the sector, rather than a Commission-led initiative. In fact, the Commission does not intend to introduce more legislation regarding mutual recognition of qualifications in specific sectors unless requested to do so by that sector. Consequently most future arrangements are likely to be agreed in the same way as that for retailing.

Presently six million people work in states other than their own and probably five times as many are cross-frontier workers. As we have seen in East Germany (although the parallel is not meant to be wholly serious), free movement will probably exacerbate skills shortages where work conditions and reward levels are less favourable rather than relieving them. While unemployment may be somewhere around 8.5 per cent in the Community as a whole, this conceals wide variations even within countries. There are, as far as can be ascertained, no substantial pockets of skilled labour waiting to be utilized. The most probable scenario is that the unskilled and their families will by and large remain where they are, unless specifically recruited under a scheme which includes training. While environmental considerations may become more important in relation to industrial processes, this does not mean that we are going to rediscover the need for large numbers of manual labourers.

However skills at all levels will be at a premium and those possessing them will be constantly exposed to temptation to move where conditions are better. Britain could be very vulnerable under such circumstances, except where our traditional weakness in foreign languages may come to our aid. Planning and action for dealing with skills shortages is likely to continue to fall within the compass of schemes promoted by national governments, trade associations, educational establishments, or European sectional groupings. At most, the Community in the guise of the Commission can only be expected to have a coordinating role. Aspects of this coordination, together with major pump-priming, will be achieved through the EC's education and training, research and development, and other programmes.

EC funding opportunities

The European Commission's medium-term programme for vocational education and training has seven main elements:

- the free movement of persons and the recognition of their qualifications;
- the initial and continuing training of the workforce;
- university training and the ERASMUS programme;
- assessing the impact of technological change on an education and training system;
- raising the level of education systems through increased cooperation;
- promoting a European dimension in education;
- the promotion of youth exchanges.

A number of opportunities exist for education and training establishments to make applications for funding from EC programmes. Normally the EC meets 50 per cent of the cost of a particular project but in some cases 100 per cent may be paid where an educational establishment is involved. However:

- some programmes are only open to universities or research institutes;
- many of the projects have an emphasis on the involvement of industry as well as academia;
- there is a need for cross-border link-ups;
- application procedures are complicated;
- deadlines are often tight, ranging from one to four months in many cases;
- much work is involved in the preparation of the project and the application for EC support;
- the tightness of conditions can mean that not all the monies allocated can be spent, leading to the frustrating requirement to make repayments.

Not surprisingly many UK universities employ consultants to support their applications for EC funding. Details of projects are published in the 'C' and 'S' series of the *OJEC*. There is evidence to suggest that the Commission is not always quite clear what precisely they are seeking, making it desirable for either representatives of the educational establishment or its consultant to visit Brussels to seek clarification.

The challenge to vocational education

The creation of the Single European Market and the move towards the creation of a European Economic Space offers providers of vocational education and training with a set of major challenges in the face of a serious national risk. There is risk that we shall not wake up to the importance of education and training in the field of work and do something practical to improve our national performance until it is too late. West Germany has a 20 per cent share of the world trade in goods with a higher skills contact; Japan has 17 per cent; the USA 15 per cent. The UK retains only a 6 per cent share and stands in danger of producing goods which are either obsolete or non-competitive. The French, with only a 7 per cent share, are already building a vocational element into university courses which are themselves accessible as a right to any prospective student holding an International Baccalaureate qualification.

Already one in three graduate vacancies of which the Central Services Unit in Manchester is notified contain a European element. That proportion will almost certainly increase. The challenge is to train people who are capable of filling both these jobs and the many others which become available during the 1990s. Having trained them, business has the separate challenge of providing the career structure and conditions which will both attract and retain them. The market place for vocational education and training in the 1990s would seem to have both a European and local dimension. While there will be a need to keep in touch with the UK government departments and perhaps even the Commission to obtain advance notice of programmes and funding opportunities, there will be an equal need to liaise with Training and Enterprise Councils and with local organizations representing both employers and unions. Only in this way will providers of vocational education and training be able to identify needs, provide the required courses and subsequently monitor and evaluate the effectiveness of their provision.

References

Cecchini, P (1988) *1992 and the Benefits of a Single European Market*, Wildwood House, Aldershot

PART II

Vocational Education – Responding to the Challenge of Europe

Introduction

The following five chapters offer a coordinated framework for a vocational educational response to the challenge of Europe. Chapter three considers the competing clients and markets served by institutions offering vocational education and proposes an educational strategy for Europeanization developed within an overarching philosophy of liberal vocationalism. This strategy is transposed to the institutional level through a model for enhancing Europeanized learning opportunities with three interacting dimensions: the curriculum; the culture, structure and processes of the institution together with its strategic and operational management; and the human resource available to it. Each of these dimensions is explored in detail in chapters four to seven.

3 Towards an Educational Strategy for Europeanization

Introduction

The implications of the Single European Market will place an onus on educational managers and practitioners to develop an educational strategy for Europeanization which can inform and structure the responses they offer. Such a strategy will need to be informed by a recognition of the clients served by vocational education and the range of markets seeking curriculum and product development. In recognizing the potential conflicts in meeting the needs of identified client groups and markets, this chapter will offer a unified educational approach which brings together humanistic concepts of education as a liberating process with the requirement of vocational education to support economic activity and development.

The preceding two chapters identified a number of significant implications arising from the Single European Market. They focused deliberately on broad economic implications and identified the role required of vocational education in meeting the requirements of employers in a context of enhanced international competition, demographic change and current and predicted skill shortages. It is axiomatic that the products of vocational education must respond to the articulated demands of clients. However in offering an informed and positive response to the implications of the Single European Market vocational education is faced with competing, and in some cases paradoxical, demands from its clients.

Competing clients of vocational education

Three broad sets of clients of vocational education may be identified: central or local government or associated agencies such as the Polytechnic and Colleges Funding Council and Training and Enterprise Councils; employers; and students. It can be argued that at a superordinate level the ultimate client of vocational education may be seen to be the party who pays for it, whether government, employer or student. However, it is clear that a considerable tension exists between the demands of these clients, and that this tension is intrinsic to the continuing philosophical and sociological debate about the role and function of education and training.

At the level of the state, recent policy initiatives by central government, such as the creation of the Polytechnic and Colleges Funding Council (PCFC) and the emerging Training and Enterprise Councils (TECs), may be seen to be strategic attempts to shape the role of vocational education in terms of the management of the economy through the content of its curriculum, and its responsiveness to perceived occupational needs. They may also be seen to be ideologically founded on a view of the superiority of market mechanisms in promoting improvements to the current quantity and quality of provision. In curriculum terms it is possible to identify a growing vocationalism in all areas of education and training stimulated by assessments of the economic and commercial position of the UK in international competitive markets and the inadequacies and lack of coherence of current vocational provision. This lack of coherence is the major stimulus for the rationalization and integration of vocational qualifications through the activities of the National Council for Vocational Qualifications (EDTA, 1989a, Jessup, 1989), and in Scotland by the Scottish Vocational Education Council (SCOTVEC).

There is however a major tension between the central government policy of enhancing the quantity and quality of vocational education required to meet the aspiration of a 'world class work-force' and an expressed commitment to constrain public expenditure as part of a macro-economic strategy to combat inflation. Certainly such a tension has been explicit in the comments of the chairs of a number of Training and Enterprise Councils during 1990, which have been critical of the reduced level of funding available to them in comparison with anticipated levels. Equally, measures to increase the student participation rate in higher education may be seen to be at variance with government policies which seek to transfer the costs of provision from the public to the private purse through mechanisms such as enhanced student fees and student loan arrangements (Barr, 1987).

At a minimum, initiatives to increase full-time participation in any form of post-compulsory education may be seen to be in conflict with the immediate recruitment practice of employers – larger employers in particular – who have sought to recruit from the dwindling supply of school leavers by offering enhanced reward and training packages and in some instances scholarship arrangements for young people in their final compulsory years at school (Lees, 1990). This pattern of enhanced competition to recruit school leavers both between education and training providers and between educational institutions and employers has, certainly since the mid-1980s, had a marked impact on the organizational structures of institutions and on the curriculum opportunities they offer. This can best be seen in the organizational structures of institutions of further and higher education and in particular the growth of:

- organizational sub-sets to manage the burgeoning youth training and employment training markets particularly during the mid- to late 1980s;
- the growth of marketing and other 'point of entry' organizational sub-sets designed to secure market research information and promote a positive institutional image to prospective clients;
- the growth of curriculum development units or similar sub-sets designed to coordinate product development in institutions and facilitate research, consultancy and similar activities, often linked to an institutional role for staff development;
- and critically, the application of more managerial forms of organizational design, many of which are based on a matrix model to promote both responsiveness and flexibility (James et al, 1989).

These essentially market-led developments have been reinforced and extended by the requirements of the 1988 Education Reform Act.

Employers have a vested interest in the UK having a competent and well-trained workforce. However, this does not appear to provide the necessary incentive for them to offer financial support to vocational education. Indeed there is evidence to suggest that there is a positive disincentive to invest in vocational education among employers, given the potential for employee 'poaching' as a viable alternative strategy (EDTA, 1989b). This reveals a tension between representative bodies of employers such as the Confederation of British Industry (CBI) and the Institute of Directors and the views of individual employers competing for a declining pool of new entrants into the labour market.

The challenge is to find a mechanism by which the macro-level requirements for an educated and vocationally competent work-force can be mediated through the recruitment and training policies and practices of employers. This will require a longer-term view of the value to the economy of young entrants into the labour market, and in particular the value of a broad-based and wide-ranging initial education. Equally it will need a reassessment of the value of non-traditional labour groups such as women returners, numbers of black and other ethnic minorities and people with disabilities.

While this will constitute a major task for employer representatives such as the CBI, and critically the emerging Training and Enterprise

Councils, the direct consequences of this tension are likely to be experienced by institutions offering vocational education. In particular the employer-led governing bodies of institutions and their senior managers may find themselves in the invidious position of mediating through their curriculum and marketing strategy a conflict between the long-term needs of the economy for an educated and competent workforce and the short-term needs of employers to meet immediate labour and skill shortages. This mediation is likely to reveal itself in the relative balance between full-time and part-time opportunities offered, and between traditional patterns of service delivery and those offered to employers and others through consultancy, professional short course provision and research activity.

Students are the client group most intricately involved with the educational process. The individual student is for many educationalists the legitimate client of vocational education, and clearly there is a complex interaction between the delivery of education and training and the quality of the student experience. (Müller and Funnell, 1991). While central and local government may create the strategic context in which vocational education is delivered, and while employers may articulate specific demands and provide major inputs both into curriculum design and the funding of provision, the fundamental outcomes of vocational education should be a series of enhancements of the competences and capability of the individual, thereby making the student both the product of, and a partner in, the educational process.

From limited competence to core skills

It is possible to view vocational education in terms of the knowledge and skills required successfully to undertake particular occupational tasks delivered through input-driven techniques, such as programmed learning without consideration of the more holistic development of a range of transferable interpersonal skills and a commitment to self-motivated learning. Indeed it is possible to criticize the competency-based model of vocational education developed by the National Council for Vocational Qualifications (NCVQ) in these terms, although this would ignore the Council's own recognition of the value of common learning outcomes, and its primary concern for the assessment of attained competence rather than the process by which it is attained.

More significantly this narrow focus on occupational competence is at variance with views expressed by a wide range of prominent bodies including the National Curriculum Council (NCC), The Confederation of British Industry (CBI), The Trade Union Congress (TUC), the Business and Technician Education Council (BTEC) and the Schools

Examination and Assessment Council (SEAC). All of these bodies support curriculum enhancement designed to generate a range of transferable core skills which will equip the individual for the world of work and facilitate the development of vocational competence.

The NCC identifies six core skills: communication; problem solving; personal skills; numeracy; information technology; and modern language competence. The recognition of the importance of modern language competence is particularly welcome in the context of the Single European Market. The NCC also recommends that emphasis be given to ensuring continuity across the whole educational system and in offering maximum progression opportunities for students. In this respect the NCC encourages the development of credit accumulation and transfer schemes to bridge the unnecessary divide between academic and vocational education (NCC, 1990).

The CBI's report *Towards A Skills Revolution* (CBI, 1989) also promotes a broader approach to post-16 vocational education. The CBI report expresses the need for a broader view of vocational competence than that being developed by the NCVQ, one which will support the development of a work-force able to adjust to economic and technological change. Central to the CBI's view is a notion of 'careerships' which focuses on the individual student pursuing a structured programme of vocational education through the mechanism of a personal action plan.

The CBI's approach has significantly informed the pilot training credit schemes to commence in 12 local education authorities in 1991. In each of these pilots an action plan for each participating 16- or 17-year-old school leaver will be drawn up by the LEA's careers service and on the basis of this plan a credit to a given financial value will be issued. In the majority of cases this credit will be managed by the young person's employer who in turn will provide vocational education in response to targets identified in the action plan. This is in line with a number of the recommendations in *Towards a Skills Revolution*. However, whether it meets the CBI's aim of encouraging a higher level of employer investment in vocational education and work-based learning through the development of a 'training market', and its ambitious targets for increased participation in education and training, must be a matter of debate. Certainly the allocation of a training credit is likely to increase critically the demand for vocational education from among that approximately one-third of all school leavers who enter the labour market and currently receive either no training or training lasting less than one year (EDTA, 1989a).

A training credit also has the potential of empowering the individual to select a set of education and training products appropriate for his or her needs. However, these advantages are likely to be balanced both by a commercial incentive for employers to provide or promote training related to the individual's immediate work role and tasks, and by an absence of continuing counselling and guidance either within employer organizations or institutions offering vocational education. It is however recognized that many institutions are actively reviewing and enhancing their pre- and post-admissions support both in response to the demand for NVQs and as part of their more general marketing strategy.

Nonetheless this does not detract from the view that without considerable change the training credits scheme is unlikely to meet the CBI proposed targets that all 16- and 17-year-olds should be eliminated from the labour market by 1992, that all young people should attain NVQ level 2 by 1995, and that by the year 2000 half the age group should have reached NVQ level 3, which is equivalent to 'A' level entry to degree level higher education. While commendable, these targets demand a significant change in the pace of development of NVQs and in the formation of 'generic units' which offer a breath of educational experience almost certainly beyond the original remit of the NCVQ, as well as the development of training infrastructures within employing organizations supported by accredited workplace trainers. In the absence of these the targets may not be met.

Given the implications of the Single European Market this becomes a double blow as the completion of these ambitious targets would still place the UK behind a number of its major economic competitors in the provision of vocational education. Further, these national developments need to be seen in the context of those being undertaken by other EC member states not least the French where changes in the baccalaureate examination has led to marked increases in 16- to 19-year-old attainment rates. Indeed the very success of the French system has put enormous pressure on the higher education sector in the country leading to a government announcement in June 1990 of an additional 16 billion franc investment in university development and renovation between 1991 and 1995 including an extra 30,000 student residences and 35,000 more study places in university libraries. President Mitterrand is quoted as having viewed this additional investment as: 'indispensable to provide France with the means of education, training and research which will guarantee our future and which is the corner-stone of our businesses' (Geddes, 1990).

This development needs to be seen within a context of overcrowded higher education provision in France, due to enormous post-war expansion to a current 1.4 million students, more than double the UK total and some 32 per cent of the age group. The expansion is planned to continue to reach a figure of some two million by the year 2000, largely as a consequence of the French Government's target to facilitate 80 per cent of young people attaining the baccalaureate while maintaining open access to higher education for those reaching this level. This explicit encouragement of post-compulsory education, equally observable in the Federal Republic of Germany (Munch, 1982), is significantly greater than offered in the UK (EDTA, 1989a).

From core skills to capability

Nonetheless, the consensus forming around the value of curriculum enhancement in the UK is encouraging action to extend both the breadth and flexibility of learning, so supporting the development of generic vocational and interpersonal skills rather than, or in addition to, those which meet the narrower needs of a specific occupational task. However this emphasis on curriculum enhancement may not, of itself, be sufficient to promote student autonomy. In this context autonomy may be defined in terms of the student's 'ownership' of his or her own learning (Boud, 1988). This approach is most explicit in the UK in the Royal Society of Arts-sponsored Education for Capability Movement.

> Central to Education for Capability is the conviction that excellence in the pursuit of knowledge should be combined with an equal regard for the capacity to get things done; to organise and design; to use and communicate knowledge – to give students opportunities to explain what they are about; to work effectively, both independently and with other people; to be enterprising, creative and imaginative. Education for capability encourages methods of teaching and learning which generate the skills and qualities which give learners opportunities to be responsible for their own learning and to relate their studies to their own development and to the world in which they live. (HECM, 1990, p. 1)

Given the requirement for an entrepreneurial response to the implications of the Single European Market by UK industry and commerce, the development of student autonomy and a propensity for self-motivated lifelong learning will be prerequisites of success. In this context, institutions offering vocational education will need to explore the tension between meeting prospective student demands for technical updating with the requirement to develop capability. How this tension is mediated through curriculum design and teaching and learning strategies will constitute a major institutional challenge, one discussed more fully in Chapter 5. Any such resolution is likely to require a continuing dialogue with employers and their representatives.

Competing markets for vocational education

Three broadly segmented markets for vocational education may be identified, the products for which need to be reviewed and enhanced to take account of the implications of the Single European Market. These are: full- and part-time qualificatory provision; the updating and retraining of work-experienced adults; and provision for non-traditional groups. While not mutually exclusive each will be considered briefly before embracing them within an educational strategy for Europeanization.

There is likely to be an increased market demand in all areas of full-time vocational education for an enhanced European focus in the curriculum. The extent and nature of this Europeanization of the curriculum will depend in part on the underpinning academic discipline or nature of the vocational area concerned, the process of curriculum review and evaluation operating in any particular institution, and the existing competence of staff. It is reasonable to assume that with the growth of a European dimension as part of an increasingly vocationally-orientated process of compulsory education, particularly through the GCSE but also through the introduction of BTEC courses and the International Baccalaureate, students will have an expectation of, and will demand, the continuity of this European focus in the post-compulsory curriculum. This notion of continuity in the curriculum is one which underpins the extension of the Technical and Vocational Education Initiative (TVEI) and is explicit in the resolution of the Council of the European Community and the Ministers of Education of the Member State on the European dimension in education, dated 24 May 1988. The objectives of this resolution are:

... to strengthen the European dimension in education by launching a series of concerted measures for the period 1988–1992; these measures should help to

– strengthen in young people a sense of European identity and make clear to them the value of European civilization and of the foundations on which the European peoples intend to base their development to date, that is in particular the safe-guarding of the principles of democracy, social justice and respect for human rights (Copenhagen Declaration, April 1978);
– prepare young people to take part in the economic and social development of the Community and in making concrete progress towards European union, as stipulated in the European Single Act;
– make them aware of the advantages which the Community represents, but also of the challenges involved in opening up an enlarged and social area to them;
– improve their knowledge of the Community and its Member States in their historical, cultural, economic and social aspects and bring home to them the significance of the cooperation of the Member States of the European Community and with other countries of Europe and the World. (OJEC, 1988)

This demand for a European dimension in the curriculum has not, and will not, be concentrated solely in areas of full-time provision. Indeed, given the immediacy of the implications of the Single European Market curriculum relevance will only be assured if these implications are fully taken into account throughout all full- and part-time provision, and not only in knowledge-based areas such as those most closely associated with the harmonization of technical standards. In practice it is likely to be in the area of part-time provision, and within it that area increasingly associated with PICKUP-type provision (professional, industrial and commercial updating) where significant additional demand has, and will continue, to occur. Indeed recent DES figures show an estimated 20 per cent increase in the numbers enrolling on updating courses in colleges, polytechnics and universities during 1987–8 compared with the previous year (DES, 1990). The major areas of updating are management development, business skills, engineering, computing and information technology, with demand for these predicted to grow together with quality assurance and language provision.

It would also seem reasonable to anticipate an increased demand from employers for research, consultancy and other products stimulated by the implications of the Single European Market. This increased demand reflects the success of the DTI's 1992 awareness raising campaign and the Department of Education and Science's own PICKUP initiative with its network of regional development agents. However while this increased demand is entirely welcome in a context of previous under-investment in vocational education, particularly during the period following the UK's entry into the EC, it represents a major set of challenges for institutions offering this provision, as will be discussed later in this text.

Nonetheless with some 80 per cent of the work-force of the year 2000 currently in employment, and with enhanced international competition and the pace of technological development in industrial and commercial practice, it will be essential that employers respond to the challenge by giving greater priority to human resource development so as to encourage staff recruitment and retention. This moves from being exhortation to commercial necessity when it is recognized that alongside the absolute decline in the numbers of 16- to 24-year-olds available to the labour market, the group which traditionally has been the conduit through which new commercial practices and styles of working have been introduced into the workplace, there will be an increase in the numbers of older workers available, especially those aged between 45 and 54. This absolute and proportionate increase in the number of older workers in the workforce, while ameliorating the potential shortage of supply of labour over the next decade, intensifies the need for vocational updating and retraining.

Individuals within this age category are likely to have experienced one or more of the following: minimal schooling during formative years; a relatively high incidence of unemployment due to structural changes in the economy resulting in skills obsolescence; skills obsolescence as a result of time out of paid employment undertaking child care responsibilities;

and little or no vocational education while in employment. Responding to this institutions offering vocational education will need to provide training and retraining programmes which employ an appropriate range of teaching and learning strategies focused on the needs of individuals to develop both vocational competence and capability.

An innovative lead in this might be expected at the local level by the emerging Training and Enterprise Councils, given their ability to bring together the consumers and producers of vocational education through a coordinated range of enterprise initiatives and training programmes. A lead might also be anticipated from industrial training boards and the industry lead bodies determining the work-based competences which form the basis of NVQs, together with others such as validating bodies. Nonetheless much of the initiative for human resource updating and retraining must of necessity come directly from employers. Combined, these factors imply a major marketing task for institutions offering vocational education with knock-on effects on the curriculum, institutional management and staff development.

Recent predictions suggest, acknowledging the uncertainty about the economic implications of the Single European Market (Hancock, in this text), that the UK will enjoy a relatively balanced labour market position over the remainder of the 1990s with the increased demand for labour being met by an overall increase in the supply of those who are economically active (Rajan, 1990). These labour-supply predictions are based on the increased participation of women, particularly those returning to work after periods of child care, and members of ethnic minority groups and people with disabilities who may currently be found disproportionately among the unwaged and unemployed both in the UK and elsewhere within the EC.

While this quantitative analysis raises a wide range of issues concerning the impact of new technology on employment practice, not least on the growth of part-time and non-traditional styles of work, the recruitment practices of employers and the application of equal opportunities policies, such participation in the labour market does provide significant opportunities to enhance the access of the non-traditional groups into vocational education. Critically they provide the economic imperative to underpin the more humanistic arguments supporting the access movement in further and higher education. This view is explicit in the report of the National Advisory Body for Public Sector Higher Education (NAB) *Action for Access* which both offers a range of recommendations for widening opportunities in higher education and argues that:

... the higher education system in this country is unsatisfactory in terms both of the size and the composition of its student body. In particular, women, black people and members of other minority ethnic groups, people with disabilities and many from certain socio-economic groups are using the system in disproportionately low numbers. As a result the country's work-force is being deprived of the skills and enthusiasm of highly motivated and competent groups of people who have a considerable contribution to make to the economic life of the community. (NAB, 1988, foreword)

Similar views have evolved from the Department of Education and Science REPLAN programme (FEU-NIACE, 1990). In this instance the implication of the Single European Market is likely to provide a drive towards enhanced access to, and participation in, vocational education for groups which have traditionally been under-represented in this area. It therefore provides a major opportunity for each institution offering vocational education to pursue its educational ideals, and commitment to its local community, within a context which is responsive to economic imperatives. As such it may provide a primary basis for an educational strategy for Europeanization.

Towards an Educational Strategy for Europeanization

A stereotypical view of vocational education may see it narrowly as referring to task-specific practical instruction. As such it has often been located toward the bottom of a perceived hierarchy of learning which places academic scholarship and pure research in an elevated and prestigious position. While clearly products of different intellectual and cultural traditions, this perceived polarity between a liberal/academic education and a narrowly defined vocational education is at best unhelpful and at worst a major constraint on the delivery of an effective response to the implications of the Single European Market. In this context an effective educational strategy for Europeanization will need to break down this polarity and promote a fusion of these disparate traditions.

Vocational education may be seen to comprise: 'learning activities which contribute to successful economic performance' (Hayes, 1984), and more specifically 'education for work, but more than mere training since it aims to prepare for all aspects of a social, economic and technological environment rather than just passing on task-specific skills' (Skilbeck, 1985). Clearly, a primary role of vocational education is the promotion of economic welfare through work-related and work-place learning. In this definition vocational education is considerably more than training and includes the promotion of generic skills and competences to facilitate a flexibility of mind and a positive response to change. This tension between liberal education and vocational education has been identified by Rust and Seabrooke as a causal factor in the relative underprovision of the latter in the UK and its status as a 'lower order of activity than education'. They go on to suggest that differences

> . . . between education and training have been emphasised and similarities and mutual interdependence denied or ignored. Powerful voices have said that it is not, and should not be, the purpose of education to have regard to the provision of a competent workforce. That education should be preparation for life is a noble enough sentiment, but quality of life for the vast majority in today's world is sustained primarily through work. Work forms a very large part of life. There should be nothing demeaning about thinking and learning about work as a part, and an important part, of life. For many people education can come through vocational competence, not the other way round'.
> (Rust and Seabrooke, 1990, p. 26)

Similar views have been expressed by Kaufman who suggests that work is a key factor in personal growth and the establishment of self-identity and self-respect. The workplace is an environment for education, one which needs to promote 'life and social skills' so as to develop habits of coping and cooperation. (FESC, 1990).

Evidence of a fusion of traditions can be found in the work of Silver and Brennan who suggest that emerging from the practicalities of curriculum development during the 1970s and 1980s is a liberal vocationalism which blends liberal and vocational traditions and allows for a range of vocational curricula differentiated in terms of their direct relationship with the labour market (Silver and Brennan, 1988). Within this context the extended use of individual learning programmes, action planning techniques and records of achievement may be seen as means by which the aspirations of the individual learner is related to given occupational needs and the status of the learner as a participant in the learning process is acknowledged and respected.

Support for the notion of a liberal vocationalism can be found in the work of Linklater who identifies the importance of information and communications technology on changing work patterns and foresees, and promotes, a situation where individual skills and 'know-how' obsolescence will be countered by a system of individual counselling and retraining in which educationalists will take a prominent role (Linklater, 1987). In Linklater's vision the process of work and continuing vocational education becomes liberating itself as opportunities for greater individual self-determination are opened up, this process occurring as a consequence of the clear interdependence of investment in developing people through vocational education (whether directly by employers or by employers coordinated by the state) and economic growth.

Within this broad philosophy of liberal vocationalism it is possible to construct an educational strategy for Europeanization which responds to the vocational needs of employers and the wider economy, while providing opportunities which empower individual students to take responsibility for their own learning, and to do so while recognizing the competition for resources and markets both within and between institutions offering vocational education. In putting such a strategy into place, institutions will need to consider three interacting dimensions: the curriculum; the culture, structure and processes of the institution, and its strategic and operational management; the human resource available to it. The relationship between these is presented in Figure 1. The model illustrated suggests that enhanced Europeanized learning opportunities will result from coordinated development in each of the three dimensions, and that while emphasis may be given to any one dimension, development and change in this area will have consequential implications for each of the other two dimensions.

This model is derived from one designed to illustrate provision development produced by the FEU (FEU, 1989).

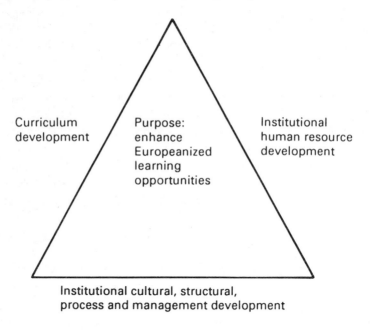

Figure 1 *Means of enhancing Europeanized learning opportunities*

Source: Derived from Further Education Unit
Toward a Framework for Curriculum Entitlement 1989

To be confident of making a quality response to the competing demands of clients and the expectations of segmented markets, an educational strategy for Europeanization will need to address the interrelated dimensions of curriculum, institutional and human resource development within an over arching philosophy of liberal vocationalism.

Economic and commercial success in responding to the implications of the Single European Market is most likely to be achieved through a liberalizing education which gives individuals increasing responsibility for their own learning. In this way the vocational competences required to close the skills and 'know-how' gaps may be acquired, while facilitating the capability of the individual to become a self-motivated lifelong learner and enjoy the richness which comes from a liberating education.

Equally this strategy creates a synergy between dominant educational traditions identifiable across the EC, which is likely to promote greater pan-European curricular integration, although the harmonization of national systems of vocational education is clearly not on the EC's political agenda at this time (Neave, 1984). Finally, and pragmatically, it is in this way that institutions offering vocational education can maintain their own economic propriety whilst providing opportunities for non-traditional and minority groups through cross-subsidized access and other provision. While offering a substantial challenge the Single European Market provides a major opportunity for the development of new patterns of liberal vocational education which will have significant benefits for the UK throughout the less insular and more explicitly European 1990s.

The following four chapters offer a discussion of each of the three dimensions represented in figure 1. Chapter 4 explores the national and international educational context within which curriculum development will occur. Chapter 5 considers curriculum development at the level of the individual institution under four broad headings: determining market needs; curriculum design; curriculum delivery and support services; evaluation. The issue of support services reappears in Chapter 6 which considers the institutional and managerial implications on an educational strategy for Europeanization. Chapter 7 considers the human resource issues for institutions offering vocational education.

References

Barr, N (1987) *The Economics of the Welfare State*, Weidenfield and Nicolson, London

Boud, D (ed) (1988) *Developing Student Autonomy in Learning*, Kogan Page, London

Brandes, D and Ginnis, P (1986) *A Guide to Student-centred Learning*, Basil Blackwell, Oxford

Confederation of British Industry (1989) *Towards a Skills Revolution*, Report of the Vocational Education Task Force, London

Department of Education and Science (1990) *Updating Britain at Work*, London

Employment Department Training Agency (1989a) *Training in Britain: The Main Report*, HMSO, London

Employment Department Training Agency (1989b) *Training in Britain: Employer's Perspectives on Human Resources*, HMSO, London

Further Education Staff College (1990) *All our Futures: Four studies of development through education and training*, Coombe Lodge Report, Blagdon

Further Education Unit (1989) *Towards a Framework for Curriculum Entitlement*

Further Education Unit and the National Institute of Adult Continuing Education (1990) *Drawing on Experience: REPLAN Projects Review*, FEU/NIACE, Rushden

Geddes, D (1990) '"Unprecedented" funds for HE expansion', *Education*, June, p. 532

Hayes, C (1984) *Competence and Competition, Training and Education in the Federal Republic of Germany, the United States and Japan*, NEDO/Manpower Services Commission, London

Higher Education for Capability Movement (1989) *Higher Education for Capability Update*, no. 1 RSA, London

James, F, Havard, B and Kershaw, N (1989) *Managing Flexible College Structures: The Current Scene*, Further Education Staff College, Blagdon, Coombe Lodge

Jessup, G (1989) 'National Vocational Qualifications: Implications for Education and Training', paper delivered at the CRAC Conference: *New Developments in Assessment and Qualifications*, Cambridge, 5–6 July 1989.

Lees, C (1990) 'Former scramble for disappearing teenagers', *The Sunday Times*, 12 August 1990, p. 7

Linklater, P (ed) (1987) *Education and the World of Work: Positive Partnership*, SRHE and Open University Press, Milton Keynes

Müller, D and Funnell, P (eds) (1991) *Delivering Quality in Vocational Education*, Kogan Page, London

Munch, J (1982) *Vocational Education in the Federal Republic of Germany*, CEDEFOP, Berlin

National Advisory Body for Public Sector Higher Education (1988) *Action for Access: Widening Opportunities in Higher Education*, NAB, London

National Curriculum Council (March 1990) *Core Skills 16–19: A Response to the Secretary of State*, NCC, York

Neave, G (1984) *The EEC and Education*, Trentham Books, Stoke on Trent

Official Journal of the European Communities (1988) 'Resolution of the Council and the Ministers of Education meeting within the Council on the European Dimension in Education', No C 177/5, 6 July

Rajan, A (1990) *1992: A Zero Sum Game*, Industrial Society, London

Rust, W B and Seabrooke, G (1990) *A European Further Education Partnership*, Association of Principals of Colleges International, Bulletin no. 2 1990, London

Silver, H and Brennan, J (1988) *A Liberal Vocationalism*, Methuen, London

Skilbeck, M (1985) *A question of quality, the Core Skills Project of the Youth Training Scheme in international perspective: Part A*, OECD, Paris

4 Promoting a Curriculum Response: the European and National Framework

The curricular response required to deliver an educational strategy for Europeanization will require two interacting components: consideration of, and response to, the broad national and international framework influencing the content and delivery of the curriculum; and more local and institutional considerations of curriculum design and the delivery of appropriate teaching and learning methods. In this chapter the broad national and international framework within which a curricular response will occur will be considered.

The European context

Vocational education systems currently in operation within member states of the EC are products of divergent historical and cultural traditions. Mclean has grouped these traditions into three generic types: encyclopaedism (with its principles of universality, rationality and utilities); humanism (with its principles of morality, individualism and specialism); and less dominant naturalist views which 'take as a starting point concepts of how individuals develop in the "real" world. They include concepts of the intellectual and moral development ... of individualism and creativity; of interaction in social groups; and of vocational commitment' (Mclean, 1990, p. 32).

Mclean argues that these competing traditions, and the diverse educational structures and systems they underpin, will be at variance with the pan-European perspective required by the implications of the Single European Market and in particular the substantial movement of people, both workers and dependent family members, across national boundaries. For Mclean this puts UK students, and within the UK particularly English students given the different cultural and educational traditions within the home countries, at a significant disadvantage. This results from a perceived weakness of the English educational system in developing competence to support workplace activities which are logical, analytical and systematic. For Mclean the exhibition of such rationality will increasingly be required in a European economy based on high-level technological production, and this will not, in his view, be supported by the currently applied form of educational individualism which is 'a very restricted phenomenon. Too often English students can only become the kind of individuals that teachers permit' (Mclean, 1990, p. 117).

The solution is:

> ... not to copy slavishly the practice of other European countries when successful transplants depend on the suitability of the soil of the recipient culture. . . A European dimension to English rationality and educational subculturalism will come inevitably as teachers, parents and children move across the Continent and return with non-English values in their duty-free luggage. Educational producers and consumers both will find they have much to gain from trans-Continental associations of interest. There is a need for an attitude of openness, curiosity and anticipation towards these links. In the end, each national educational culture may retain much of its own distinctiveness, which will add to the richness of Europe and to enhanced consumer choice. But distinctiveness will be accompanied by awareness of what rival cultures have to offer and by the universal acceptance of a minimum international currency of rational public knowledge. (Mclean, 1990, p. 117)

For Mclean the successful educational response to changing international market conditions and the cultural diversity of a Europe typified by the free movement of individuals, 'means above all consumer choice – that the recipients of education claim their individuality rather than have it thrust upon them' (p. 117). These views find support in the work of the Round Table of European Industrialists (RTEI) who suggest, from an explicitly commercial perspective, that educational systems based on a nationalistic concern to promote a strong cultural identity, and which emphasized national differences and not a mutual European heritage, are redundant:

> ... the situation today is not related to the requirements of nationhood or basic industrial educational needs. In a unifying Europe with a free labour market and transferability and compatibility of skills the requirements on the educational system are different. Today similarities are sought, not differences. The concept of strong nationalism has been taken over by Europeanism. Diversity and separate identity should be overcome and exchanged for educational systems which are mutually strengthening and supportive. (Kairamo, 1989, p. 16)

While there is no explicit and immediate EC policy intention to harmonize and standardize the delivery of vocational education across the Community there is a strong sense in which the implications of the Single European Market will stimulate a market-led drive towards this. Two major processes by which this may occur are: an increasing realization of the value of experimentation with, and ultimate absorption of, patterns of vocational education applied elsewhere in the Community; consumer-led demand for both the harmonization of vocational and other educational qualifications either through the direct actions of the Commission of the European Community and/or nation states, or through the individual choices of employers and students seeking qualifications which have perceived value across Europe.

It is clear that central and local government policy makers, and institutions offering vocational education, are increasingly recognizing the value of exploring and, where useful, adopting models of vocational education prevalent in the EC. Within the UK the Federal Republic of Germany's 'dual system' with its interaction of State and employer activity has been identified as an example of good and interesting practice (Casey, 1990). This trend is explicit in the White Paper *Employment for the 1990s* (CM540, 1988) which in addition to identifying 'demography, global competitive forces, and the changing nature of employment itself' (p. 5) as representing major drives towards a changed approach to 'preparing today's workers for tomorrow's jobs', (p. 6) also recognizes that significant lessons can be learnt from the UK's international competitors:

> There is no simple model which could be borrowed from any of our competitors to help us solve our own problem. Each of our competitors has developed an approach to suit its own needs. Those that do best have developed training and vocational education systems which reach the majority of the population.
>
> At the outset of life they teach and expect high standards across a broad range of subjects. They value practical competences as well as theoretical knowledge. They have a belief in continuing education and training through life. Above all training and vocational education is treated as an essential commercial investment on a par with research and development.
>
> Several countries, notably Germany and the United States, also have more locally based training systems with a close and continuous involvement with employers and employer institutions. Such systems are much more likely to be attuned to the shifting pattern of employer needs, and to individuals requirements, and the more inflexible arrangements of national and industry levels. It is at the local level that jobs and a need for particular skills arise. It is at the local level that people live and work who would wish to be trained for new and changing jobs. (CM540, 1988, p. 29)

There is considerable range and variety in the systems and structures of vocational education offered in each of the 12 member states of the European Community (Johnson, 1989). Differences exist in the age at which compulsory education ceases; the range and type of post-compulsory education offered; the relationship between vocational education and that which has a predominantly academic basis; the extent of involvement of social partners (in particular employers and trade associations) in the provision and accreditation of vocational education; and the availability of access routes into higher education. As previously discussed these differences may be seen to reflect national economic priorities and cultural traditions: however, the very variety and richness of these national systems may operate against the economic logic of a single market, particularly one which encourages labour mobility and the offering of professional and business services across national boundaries. Equally different assessments of the quality of provision offered in each member state, and the value of resultant qualifications, has and will continue to mitigate against the efficient deployment of scarce labour resources across the EC.

Comparability of vocational qualifications

Since the 1960s there have been Commission-led attempts to develop comparisons between professional occupations on a sectoral basis in different member states and the vocational education associated with these occupations. The initial objective of this work was to harmonize European professional qualifications. The expectation was that harmonization would itself reflect an equivalence of the learning experience of individual students, so facilitating the transferability of labour resource. However, given the methodological difficulties associated with the evaluation of comparative learning experiences as assessed by vocational qualifications, and the national and commercial vested interest which act as a disincentive to the acceptance of comparability, this approach was largely unsuccessful. That sectoral harmonization which has occurred has primarily been in health care areas covering the occupations of: doctor; general practitioner; nurses responsible for general care; midwives; dental practitioners; and pharmacists. Additionally a harmonization directive covering veterinary surgeons was passed in 1979, and a directive covering the mutual recognition of architectural qualifications, which unlike harmonization does not specify minimum levels of vocational education, was agreed in 1985 after 17 years of discussion.

This failure to agree harmonized qualifications may be seen as part of the wider set of problems associated with all forms of harmonization addressed by the Single European Act which moved politically and pragmatically to the development of a single market based on the mutual recognition of standards (Luff in this text).

Predicted levels of skills and 'know-how' shortages across the EC and throughout the 1990s has given greater urgency to the development of a mechanism for the recognition of those higher educational qualifications which lead to the awarding of professional status. Consequently the Council of Ministers passed in December 1988 a directive establishing a 'General System for the Recognition of Higher Education Diplomas' (*OJEC*, 1989a) which will enable a professionally qualified individual from one member state to become a member of the equivalent profession in another state without having to requalify. On the basis of mutual recognition a fully qualified professional in one member state is deemed to be fully qualified in any other, subject to two safeguards: that the length of education and training which the professional has received in their member state of origin is comparable with that in the other state; and there is no substantial difference in the content of education and training leading to professional recognition between the two member states.

In both cases procedures have been identified for the incoming professional to be notified of the compensatory activity he or she will be required to undertake. Operated in this way the principle and procedures of mutual recognition avoid the complexities of agreeing a common curriculum for each profession. It has been developed in the belief that any fully trained professional in a given field in likely to have much the same level of knowledge and skill as required by counterparts in other member states.

There has been some questioning of this assumption (Bemrose and Dobson in this text). At a minimum, mutual recognition will require professional bodies to have a greater depth of understanding of the vocational education provided within other member states. This will challenge the traditional insularity of many professional groups and offer particular challenges for UK professional bodies, many of whom, unlike other EC member states, are self-regulating through Royal Charter. In turn the mutual recognition of professional qualifications is likely to have significant implications for the curriculum, and modes of delivery of programmes of study leading to professional qualifications.

Clearly programmes of study which fall outside the directive, for example the current Certificate of Qualification in Social Work, or the diploma which is replacing it, will lead, directly or indirectly, to a form of professional disbarment from practice on mainland Europe. As with all other programmes of study, those leading to professional qualifications will need to be reviewed in terms of an enhanced European dimension. This will need to go beyond an awareness of the nature and extent of education and practice in other member states, and the development of language skills, to an understanding of the social patterns and culture which underpin professional practice across the EC. It will need to encourage a sensitivity to that profession's place in the social structure of other member states.

Certainly this will be the expectation of students who will need to consider the opportunities associated with professional practice on mainland Europe, and of institutions employing professionals qualified in other member states. Given this it is possible to envisage a greater market-led demand for a harmonization of vocational education leading to professional qualification in line with the greater emphasis on European patterns of recruitment envisaged for the 1990s and beyond.

Labour mobility within the single market can be anticipated in all areas of skills shortage and not solely those for which professional, or higher educational, qualifications are required. Consequently the creation of a Single European Market has also given urgency to the mutual recognition of all forms of vocational educational qualification. A substantial body of work in this field has been undertaken by the European Centre for the Development of Vocational Training (CEDEFOP) in association with national governments, training providers and others.

In response to the European Council's decision of 16 July 1985 to expedite common action by member states and the Commission to establish the comparability of vocational qualifications, a major EC study has begun and continues on a rolling programme basis (Hutchings, 1985). The key elements of this study involve: member states working together to produce mutually agreed job descriptions in given occupations and linking vocational qualifications to these job descriptions; and each member state designating a coordinating body to work with the social partners (employers and the work-force) in the appropriate occupational sectors, and to ensure information on comparability is communicated to interested parties.

In the UK this coordinating body is the Employment Department Training Agency who has responsibility for maintaining links with similar bodies from other member states and CEDEFOP. Tables of comparable qualifications have been published in the *Official Journal of the European Communities* (1989b) to cover the vocational areas of hotel and catering; motor vehicle repair and maintenance; and construction. During 1990 technical work had been completed in the areas of agricultural and electrical occupations and was underway in the areas of textile and garment manufacture, metal working occupations and office spaced occupations. The list of occupations identified by the Commission for the next round of comparability work includes those associated with the following sectors: chemicals; retail and wholesale trade; food; public works; printing; processing; the environment; tourism; woodwork; energy and health.

The comparability of national qualifications has the value of allowing prospective employers to identify whether a job applicant from one member state has the skills and competences necessary to undertake a particular job role in another member state. This is facilitated by the explicit relationship between the 'common' job description which lists elements of the job role, and the vocational qualification which demonstrates competence in those elements. However the value of this approach is limited by the inclusion in the agreed job descriptions of only those elements of the occupational task which are common across all member states. While this may be seen to represent a legitimate methodological base for assessing comparability, it restricts the practical value of the comparison to a range of technical skills, without recourse to the more qualitative core interpersonal skills discussed in Chapter 3.

For the individual job applicant the ability to demonstrate comparability of vocational qualification will only be important if the prospective employer perceives quality in the national qualification, and learning experience that underpins it, offered as a base for comparability. Indeed it is likely to be these perceptions of quality, rather than bureaucratically determined notions of comparability, which will determine the value of the qualification and the consequent employability of the applicant. Consequently the anecdotal perceptions of quality held by employers and others take on significant importance and constitute a major challenge for institutions offering vocational education.

It is a truism to state that some institutions and certain types of educational experience and qualification enjoy a higher status and profile than others. In a more intensely competitive European market for vocational education these perceptions of quality are likely to become more rather than less significant. With changes in the structure of industry and commerce, a greater European awareness and set of market opportunities for individuals to select the place and style of vocational education they receive, institutions offering vocational education are likely to experience market decline if they are perceived to offer products and services which lack quality in a European context.

Occupational standards and NVQs

There has developed a strong relationship between the development of occupational standards, the reform of vocational qualifications through the NCVQ, and attempts to identify comparable vocational qualifications across the EC. Occupational standards, precise descriptions of what employees are expected to be able to do, are based on an analysis of a given occupational area carried out by members of the relevant industrial lead body, with professional assistance. In the UK the intention of the EDTA's Standards Programme is to facilitate ownership of these standards by industry to encourage their subsequent application. Also, and critically, once agreed the assessment components of occupational standards can, with the support of recognized examining and validating bodies, be developed into a qualification. This can in turn be submitted to the NCVQ for recognition as part of the national framework of vocational qualifications.

Despite the slow pace of activity towards a national framework of

NVQs, most clearly demonstrated in the high number of conditional accreditations awarded up to August 1990, there remains considerable optimism within the NCVQ that this model of determining and accrediting occupational competence and vocational qualifications will have wide-ranging impact across the EC:

> The Government's intention is that all national qualifications which relate to the employability of an individual, including professional qualifications, should be classified within the NVQ framework. This will greatly strengthen our position in making comparisons with European systems. Britons travelling abroad will be armed with qualifications, showing the competences held by the holder, which will be readily understood by Europeans. The NVQ computerized database will provide a comprehensive source of all qualifications and their constituent competences. One can foresee the development in the 1990s of a European database which extends the NVQ model. A competence-based form of qualification provides the best expression of what holders of the qualification can actually do. (Jessup, 1989)

While this might be seen as somewhat self-congratulatory, it is clear that the new competence-based vocational qualificatory system developing in the UK, founded on explicit occupational standards, does offer a meaningful alternative to that available in a number of other member states. Further, by concentrating on occupational competence it provides the basis for a more sophisticated method of assessing the comparability of vocational qualifications across the EC than that currently being developed.

That there is no mainland European equivalent to NVQ level one must be seen as both an advantage and disadvantage – a disadvantage in that it has the potential to perpetuate the low level of vocational educational aspiration in the UK which has been the hallmark of the national failure to train. However it may also represent an advantage in that it does offer a nationally recognized qualificatory target which is achievable by virtually everyone, and which when successfully achieved may encourage further vocational education based on success. So, while much of the competence accredited under NVQ level one may be regarded as pre-vocational, the existence of this level does serve to provide opportunities to encompass virtually everyone within the national framework based on merit. This may also have the advantage of reducing perceptions of inferiority which could be applied to qualifications which lie outside the national framework.

This analysis does suggest the existence of a humanistic element within the NVQ framework which can be seen to be at variance with the more severely meritocratic vocational education systems operated by other EC member states (see, for example, Eurydice 1986). This also suggests that the NVQ framework does have the potential to balance both the commercial and economic requirements for standardized qualifications with the more humanistic requirement to promote educational attainment and facilitate lifelong learning based on success.

The fulfilment of this aspiration will, however, require a clear consensus on the definition of the key concept of 'competence'. The NCVQ has defined competence as 'the ability to perform work activities to the standards required in employment' (NCVQ, 1988). It has defined a statement of competence as one which incorporates specific standards in 'the ability to perform in a range of work-related activities, and the underpinning skills, knowledge and understanding required for performance in employment' (NCVQ, 1989 p. 4). The Employment Department Training Agency has extended the definition of competence to be:

... the ability to perform the activities within an occupation. Competence is a wide concept which embodies the ability to transfer skills and knowledge to new situations within the occupational area. It encompasses organization and planning of work, innovation and coping with non-routine activities. It includes those qualities of personal effectiveness that are required in the workplace to deal with co-workers, managers and customers. (Debling, 1990)

The assimilation of the management of technical and task components with the management of the unpredictable, and the integration of an occupational role within the wider organizational, economic and social context, are significant elements of this broader definition. Again this reinforces the demand for individual capability based on curricula enhancement and learner autonomy. This concept of competence reinforces the educational strategy for Europeanization developed in Chapter 3. It also poses significant challenges for institutions offering vocational education in developing specific curricular responses to the implications of the Single European Market.

EC research programmes

A further component of the international framework influencing the curricula responses of individual institutions are the programmes of research and training funded by the Commission of the European Community, together with the availability of other forms of structural funding.

A complex set of EC research programmes exist which are primarily concerned with the development and application of technology. The Second Framework Programme which runs from 1987 to 1991 covers eight priority areas subdivided into specific programmes. The Third Framework Programme agreed in December 1989 will overlap the second and is intended to promote continuity. The eight priority areas are: quality of life (including health, radiation protection and environmental issues);

information and communication technologies; industrial technologies; bio-technology; energy; science and technology for development; marine technologies; improvement of European science and technology development.

Specific programmes within these areas range from the enormous European Strategic Programme for Research and Development in Information Technologies (ESPIRIT II) with its EC contribution between 1987 and 1992 of ECU 1,600 million, to much smaller ones such as Science and Technology for Environmental Protection and European Programme on Climatology and Natural Hazards (STEP-EPOCH), with an EC contribution of ECU 115 million. The ESPIRIT II programme is particularly large, demonstrating the priority given by the Commission to the development of basic technologies for the European information technology industry and the promotion of European industrial cooperation in pre-competitive research and development in this business area.

The Commission's research strategy is based on the perceived value of research in pursing the objectives of the Single European Market:

> The prospect of a single internal market in 1992 . . . represents a great challenge for companies in all fields of training and industry. It offers a unique opportunity to cut costs, expand markets, rationalise and exploit new potential. This applies as much to research, technology and innovation as to business aspects such as cost structure, market positioning and export capability. . . The main aim [of the research strategy] is to maintain and strengthen the international competitiveness of European industry in high technology sectors, in the face of competition on global markets, above all from the USA and Japan . . . [and to promote] more transparency, information and coordination to avoid duplication of effort and to promote cooperation and synergy. . . However EC research promotion must not be perceived simply as a new source of subsidies. The overall concept of research work is much more important; here financial aid is only one element, and by no means the most crucial. The successful project at EC level will depend on its real innovative value. (CEC, 1990, p. 3)

Consequently the major aims of the Commission's research policy are to promote:

- cross-border cooperation, coordination and mobility between industry and science;
- the undertaking of basic research, an increasingly important area of activity and one which small and medium-sized companies rarely have the necessary personnel or capital to undertake independently;
- the integration of research and technology to support the completion of the Single European Market, especially in the area of the mutual recognition of standards.

There is a paucity of evidence to demonstrate either the level or extent of participation in these research programmes by UK institutions, although anecdotally it would seem that participation has been primarily within the university sector, the larger polytechnics or consortium bodies such as Regional Technology Centres. This pattern of participation is likely to reflect the entrepreneurial approach exhibited by institutions and their national and international reputation in pure and applied research. Again, anecdotally, it would seem that where other institutions have become involved in research projects it is as a consequence of explicit competence in a specific, and often narrow, area of activity, or based on the entrepreneurial activities of one or more individuals within the institution rather than as a result of an explicit institutional research policy.

EC programmes to support vocational education

Of major importance to institutions offering vocational education is the battery of programmes designed to support education and training initiatives. Of these, three are of particular importance: the European Action Scheme for the Mobility of University Students (ERASMUS), the second phase of which, ERASMUS II, commenced in 1990; the Community Action Programme in Education and Training for Technology (COMETT), the second phase of which, COMETT II, also commenced in 1990; and the LINGUA programme promoting foreign language knowledge within the EC which begins a pilot phase in 1990.

The basis for the ERASMUS programme was created by decisions of the European Council of 15 June 1987 and 14 December 1989 (*OJEC* 1987,1989d). The objectives of the ERASMUS programme may be summarized as:

- to increase significantly the number of students spending a fully recognized period of study in another Community country;
- to promote broad-based, cooperative activities between universities in all member states;
- to improve the quality of education offered by universities in each member state by pooling the intellectual skills of teaching staff through increased mobility;
- to promote closer contact among Europeans to support the development of a 'people's Europe';
- to support the development of trained personnel able to enter the graduate labour market with direct experience of at least one other member state.

For the purpose of the ERASMUS programme the term 'university' is used to describe all types of higher education institutions which are either within the state sector or recognized or financed by the state. This is irrespective of the designation given to the institution within the member state.

To support meeting these objectives the ERASMUS programme groups activities under four 'actions', namely:

- Action One – the establishment and operation of a European university network through support for inter-university cooperation programmes (ICPs) and study visits;
- Action Two – the ERASMUS student grants scheme;
- Action Three – measures to promote mobility through the academic recognition of diplomas and periods of study;
- Action Four – complementary measures to promote student mobility across the Community.

During 1988–89 the programme had available a total budget of ECU 52.5 million and activity was concentrated in the following areas:

- the launch of the pilot phase of the European Community Course Credit Transfer System (ECTS). A six-year pilot scheme designed to provide a means by which students undergoing or having completed higher education may receive credit for learning carried out at any of the ECTS partner institutions. As such it is a scheme based on mutual trust between the participating institutions. This pilot scheme will be operating over a six-year period from the academic year 1989–90 to 1994–95;
- the continued evaluation of ERASMUS I activities leading to modifications in ERASMUS II;
- the continuation of dissemination activities;
- the consolidation of the organizational and administrative aspects of the programme.

Evaluating the ERASMUS programme Absalom suggests that:

> ... it may fairly be said that by the end of 1989 ERASMUS had, in relation to the resources available to it, developed its maximum potential both quantitatively and qualitatively, continuing to attract the interest and participation of growing numbers of staff and students in Universities and other higher education institutions throughout the Community. The fact that the Programme supported almost 5,000 inter-university cooperation agreements involving the mobility of some 80,000 students over the four years of its existence alone suffices to make the point. (Absalom, 1990, p. 39)

For Absalom 'ERASMUS ... is a means, and not an end'. It can provide stimulus for innovation and the reform and restructuring of the curriculum. However it also carries the danger of distorting curriculum development and design at the level of the institution. This results as a consequence of the increasing competition within institutions to secure external forms of funding leading to personal prestige for those who succeed. This 'may become an important factor in the micro-politics of the institution, and also in the career enhancement of individuals' (Absalom, 1990, p. 51).

So while a successful bid for ERASMUS support may promote individual or sectional interests it may be dysfunctional for the institution as a whole. Critical to this analysis is a recognition that any form of EC resource support may have unpredicted knock-on effects elsewhere. This may be within the curriculum or resource base of the institution, and these will certainly generate an opportunity cost-associated with the preparation required to support the initial bid. This does not negate the value of securing EC support, indeed many of these points will be true of any other similar form of development. However it does strengthen the requirement for careful initial planning and explicit institutional commitment to precede with a bid for resource support.

The European Community Action Programme for Education and Training for Technology (COMETT) was launched in 1987 to encourage investment in human resource development through training for technology and to create and strengthen networks of educational institutions and industry for this purpose. More precisely the objectives of the COMETT programme are:

- to promote a European dimension to cooperation between universities and industry and commerce in training related to innovation and change;
- to promote the joint development of training programmes and the exchange of experience and resources at EC level;
- to improve the supply of training at all levels;
- to identify and respond to training needs in technology and related areas at both member state and EC level, and promote equality of opportunity.

The first two rounds of the COMETT programme during 1987 resulted in 1,038 successful applicants from a total of 2,550. The programme itself is divided into five strands:

- strand A is concerned with the development of university enterprise training partnerships (UETPs);
- strand B(a) is concerned with student placements in industry and commerce;
- strand B(b) is concerned with exchanges between educational institutions and industry and commerce across EC boundaries;
- strand C is concerned with the development and testing of joint projects;

● strand D is concerned with the development of joint training projects.

Thompson and Ambler's evaluation of the first two rounds of the COMETT project indicate that strands A, B(a) and C generated most applications and subsequently accepted projects. They found that the majority of those participating in the programme identified net benefits arising from participation broadly in line with their expectations. However:

> . . . nearly one-third considered that they had underestimated the costs, whilst very few had over-estimated the benefits. This indicated that participants had, if anything, tended to underestimate the balance between the costs and benefits of transnational collaborative projects. The benefits from involvement in the projects were considered by survey respondents to be:
> ● new contacts for further collaboration;
> ● more effective management of collaboration, especially trans-national;
> ● improved knowledge and development of training relevant to new technologies and industrial needs. Reduced development costs and the spread of risks were not recognised by the majority of survey respondents as presented benefits of the project. (Thompson and Ambler, 1990, p. 29)

Major areas of take-up of available COMETT funding have led to the development of UETPs across the UK and a growth in student exchange arrangements between educational institutions. Where developments have occurred between educational institutions and industry and commerce these have tended to be among partners who have previously collaborated – over 70 per cent in Thompson and Ambler's research. As they conclude, this 'suggests that COMETT has mainly reached organizations that already had experience of university-industry collaboration' (p. 30).

The development of staff exchanges across the EC has tended to be relatively low and this is increasingly recognized as a function of the low level of awareness of the COMETT programme and the level of disruption to career and personal life that a lengthy exchange period in another member state can cause the individual. In their review, Thompson and Ambler concluded that while overall the development of COMETT projects could be seen to contribute to the stated objectives of the programme this conclusion was less clear when detailed work was undertaken at the level of individual strands. Indeed:

> . . . a number of areas of concern were indicated:
> ● lack of industrial awareness and involvement;
> ● the inadequate dissemination of information and best practice;
> ● insufficient market research and inadequate attention to mechanisms for marketing the outputs;
> ● low potential for self-sufficiency and self-subsigned development, particularly in strands A and B. (p. 32)

This research also identified the existence of clear relationships between COMETT and ERASMUS, and indeed other Community programmes, together with confusion within educational institutions about these relationships. Similar confusion exists between COMETT and the funding of training under the Community's social and regional funds (Teague, 1989).

Both the ERASMUS and COMETT programmes offer opportunities for trans-national collaboration and staff and student exchanges. There is sufficient evidence to suggest that such arrangements contribute to increased European awareness of participants, and that they will contribute to the development of a market-led demand for common European educational policies and standards throughout the 1990s. However it is equally clear that the allocation of funds to date has favoured entrepreneurial institutions, predominantly those in the higher education sector. This inevitably creates forms of distributive injustice in the availability of resources for students following the same programme of study in different institutions, and between types of institution offering vocational education.

Equally the very entrepreneurialism required to secure funding may mitigate against institutions adopting a strategic 'whole institutional' approach to the implications of the Single European Market. Rather it will tend to encourage a resource-led approach which ties development to specific levels of external funding. The danger of such an approach is that it can take strategic consideration away from issues of curriculum and staff development at the level of the institution and focus it narrowly on specific curriculum areas where funding is to be available.

Clearly while it is not the intention to criticize existing developments, or the entrepreneurialism that underpins them, it is important to recognize that this resource-led approach may actually restrict strategic institutional growth, and certainly puts particular initiatives at risk in situations where there is an unexpected reduction in funding or when individual members of staff leave. By comparison a strategic 'whole institutional' approach encourages the detailed review of the costs and benefits of involvement in EC-funded programmes and acts as a constraint on involvement in programmes on the basis of individual self-interest or micro-political advantage. This issue is explored more fully in Chapters 5 and 6.

The LINGUA programme which begins a pilot phase in 1990 has been designed with the key objectives of:

- promoting a quantitative and qualitative improvement in foreign language training within the EC;
- ensuring effective measures for the provision of language expertise in

the present and future work-force to support industrial and commercial enterprises across the EC in taking full advantage of the Single European Market.

In particular LINGUA is designed to:

- increase opportunities for the teaching and learning of languages in the EC in vocational training programmes, and in particular to encourage the development of less widely-used languages;
- raise the quality and standards of provision in this field by improving the initial and continuing professional development of language lecturers, teachers and trainers, including appropriate staff development on mainland Europe;
- promote innovation in methods of language teaching by the effective use of communications technologies. (*OJEC*, 1989c)

Considerable reservation was expressed by the UK Government about involvement in the LINGUA programme which was perceived to be interfering with an area of national sovereignty. This tension, subsequently resolved by pragmatic compromise, enhanced the publicity given to the LINGUA programme resulting in a high level of awareness and expressed interest in the programme. Consequently the UK LINGUA Unit was the second of the member state offices to be established and there is likely to be strong competition for the ECU 200 million available over five years from 1990. It will however be some time before it is possible to evaluate meaningfully the contribution the LINGUA programme will make to enhancing language competences.

The local dimension

What is clear is that institutions are now experiencing increased market demand for language provision reflecting, among others: trends in foreign travel; the success of the DTI's 1992 campaign; the Language Export Centre (LX) initiative funded by the DTI, DES and Employment Department Training Agency; the impact of the TVEI and other curriculum initiatives which have in particular locations developed a strong European dimension. Given this increased demand the relative importance of the LINGUA programme is diminished. Indeed the opportunity for funding curriculum development by means of cross-subsidization currently exists through the LX network, and through the provision of tailored provision on a full-cost, or profit-making basis. This example suggests that while considerable attention has been focused within vocational education on the availability of EC funding this may have been misplaced. For the majority of institutions offering vocational education the major markets for students, or consultancy and research, are local or regional. The implications of the Single European Market will be experienced critically at the local level, its impact mediated by the uniqueness of place.

This offers all institutions opportunities to research their existing and potential markets and construct programmes to meet identified needs. As such it deliberately focuses consideration of the implications of the Single European Market into the process of curriculum development within each institution. This is not intended to negate the potential value of EC funding, rather to suggest that it can be most effectively employed as part of a strategic 'whole institutional' approach which is curriculum and service-led.

This chapter has identified key elements of the European and national framework within which institutions must consider their curriculum response to the implications of the Single European Market. The importance of measures to facilitate the mutual recognition of qualifications across the EC has been stressed both in terms of underpinning perceptions of quality and market-led demand for new forms of learning opportunities. A critical review of major EC funding programmes suggests the need for a 'whole institutional' approach based on initial planning and institutional commitment. The challenge for individual institutions is to enhance Europeanized learning opportunities within this framework. Figure 1 suggested that this could be achieved by coordinated action across the three dimensions of: the curriculum; the institution's culture, structure, processes and management; and the human resource available to it. These three dimensions are explored in the subsequent chapters.

References

Absalom, R (1990) 'Practical rather than Declamatory Co-operation: ERASMUS in 1990, an appraisal', *European Journal of Education*, vol. 25, no. 1, Carfax, Abingdon

Casey, B (1990) *Recent Developments in West Germany's Apprenticeship Training System*, Policy Paper no. 1, Policy Studies Institute, London

CM 540 (1988) *Employment for the 1990's*, HMSO, London

Commission of the European Communities (1990) *EC Research Funding*, CEC, Bonn

Debling, G (1990) 'The new competence based vocational qualifications in Great Britain placed in a European context', *Competence and Assessment*, Issue 11, Employment Department Training Agency

Eurydice European Unit (1986) *The Education structures in the Member States of the European Communities*, Commission of the European Communities, Brussels

Hutchings, C (1987) 'Comparability of vocational training qualifications in the EEC', *Employment Gazette*, HMSO, June

Jessop, D (1989) Foreword to R Johnson below

Johnson, R (1989) *Vocational Qualifications in the Member States of the European*

Community and moves towards an open market, NCVQ R&D Report no. 2, NCVQ, London

Kairamo, K (ed) (1990) *Education for Life: A European Strategy*, Butterworth/Round Table of European Industrialists, Brussels

McLean, M (1990) *Britain and a Single European Market*, Kogan Page, London

National Council for Vocational Qualifications (1988) *The NVQ Criteria and Related Guidance*, NCVQ, London

National Council for Vocational Qualifications (1989) *National Vocational Qualifications: Criteria and Procedures*, NCVQ, London

Official Journal of the European Communities (1987) 'European Community Action Scheme for the Mobility of University Students (ERASMUS)', Decision 87/227/EEC of 15 June 1987

Official Journal of the European Communities (1989a) 'Council Directive of 21 December 1988 on a general system for the recognition of higher-education diplomas awarded on completion of professional education and training of at least three years' duration', no. L19/16, 24 January 1989, HMSO, London

Official Journal of the European Communities (1989b) 'Informative sheet on the comparability of vocational training qualifications between the Member States of the European Community established in implementing Council Decision 85/368/EEC of 16 July 1985', no. C209/1, 14 August 1989

Official Journal of the European Communities (1989c) 'Decision of the Council of the European Community establishing the LINGUA programme 28 July 1989', no. L239/28, 16 August

Official Journal of the European Communities (1989d) 'European Community Action Scheme for the Mobility of University Students, Decision of the Council of the European Communities 89/663/EEC of the 14 December 1989, no. L395

Teague, P (1989) *The European Community: The Social Dimension*, Kogan Page, London, in association with Cranfield School of Management

Thompson, Q and Ambler, M (1990) 'Evaluation of the COMETT Programme', *European Journal of Education*, vol. 25, no. 1, Carfax, Abingdon

5 Delivering Curriculum Change

A context of change

In recent years institutions offering vocational education have been required, and many have actively sought, to review and develop their institutional curricula in line with the requirements and encouragement of external bodies such as the Employment Department Training Agency and validating bodies such as BTEC or the Council for National Academic Awards (CNAA) or support and advisory bodies such as the FEU and the Further Education Staff College (FESC). In most cases the promotion of curriculum review and development has been underpinned by an attempt to enhance the degree of vocationalism in the curriculum. Such developments have sought to go beyond a minimalist view of vocationalism to encompass areas of core interpersonal skills, and as such reflect elements of the liberal vocationalism discussed in Chapter 3. It is within this context of change that institutions offering vocational education will need to place emphasis on the process and product of curriculum review and development in the light of the implications of the Single European Market.

Critical to this will be a realization that these implications will permeate the whole curriculum of institutions and will not be constrained within particular sub-sets of that curriculum. This suggests the need for curriculum audit and review to ascertain the degree of enhancement required. Equally it must be recognized that different aspects of curriculum change will be required by the various competing markets served by institutions offering vocational education: full- and part-time qualificatory; updating and retraining of work-experienced adults; and provision for non-traditional groups.

There is anecdotal evidence to suggest that many of the curricula initiatives developed in response to the implications of the Single European Market have been based on the entrepreneurial activities of individuals within institutions, often linked to the acquisition of external sources of funding (Funnell, 1990; Bonney in this text). This suggests that developments have occurred in an uncoordinated way within institutions with the likelihood of unproductive duplication and inefficient overlap of provision both within and between individual institutions. Indeed in recognition of this one of the primary tasks of the DES-funded PICKUP Europe Unit, set up in 1990, is the dissemination of information about the current practice within the UK further and higher education sectors so as to minimize these inefficiencies. However the activities of external bodies may do little to lessen the potential for unproductive duplication or overlap existing within single institutions. This emphasizes the need for a 'whole institutional' approach to curriculum development based on a clear development model and an explicit commitment to change.

The term 'curriculum' is used here not to describe a range of subjects or topic areas in a single programme of learning, or to describe the content taught in any one of these subject or topic areas, but rather the totality of provision offered by an institution to its students. It describes all that learning which is planned and guided by an institution, whether undertaken in groups or individually, inside or outside the physical buildings and facilities of the institution (Kerr, 1968). This use of the term has been extended by the FEU into a vocational educational setting:

> . . . the curriculum is more than merely a set of subjects, a syllabus or course; it is also more than the content of a particular learning programme. Curriculum involves all those processes which facilitate, or if they go wrong, inhibit learning. It thus can be seen to include the means of recruitment to a programme and progression from it, the ethos of a learning institution and learning styles, in addition to content. (FEU, 1989)

The successful progress of curriculum development will involve a number of interacting components:

- an assessment of market needs and demands mediated by the views and judgements of managers and members of staff of the institution in relation to operational constraints and opportunities, and the over-arching corporate statement of purpose (or mission statement) of the institution;
- the design of learning programmes at which stage the competing demands and expectations of clients are brought together into coherent learning packages;
- the delivery of learning programmes by the application of appropriate teaching and learning strategies and the availability of effective support services;
- the review and evaluation of interactions with vocational education.

Understanding market needs

An essential prerequisite of an effective curricular response will be an understanding of the needs and demands of the clients and market segments to be supported by vocational education. The systematic collection, storage and retrieval of information will become increasingly important as institutions shape their services and products in response to change. Institutions will be driven by their own requirements for commercial survival to develop increasingly sophisticated forms of market research so as to inform the whole institution of potential areas of new product development and the adjustment or revision of existing provision. This goes beyond that which might be associated with a 'responsive college' (Bilbrough et al, 1988) to one which is essentially pro-active, predicting future needs and experimenting with new product development to meet that predicted need. As Stanton suggests:

> . . . a college can be pro-active and promote industrial growth in its area by providing a vocational education infrastructure. There are, for instance, colleges around where there are clusters of small studios for design and other services. The small businesses are there because the college is there, and that is where the employers and employees come from. They stayed in the area they knew, with the contacts they had, because they knew that training and retraining could be provided by the college. (Stanton, 1989, p. 25)

However the effective development of the 'pro-active college' will require marketing strategies which go beyond the collection and summation of secondary data sources to the creation of networks and relationships with employers, representative bodies and others within given localities to ensure the efficient collection of primary data. Mechanisms will then be required to ensure that such primary data is available to the whole institution and does not remain the preserve of particularly well-informed, and therefore potentially powerful, individuals within the institution. Present and past students represent a significant marketing resource both in terms of the acquisition of market information and in the promotion of the institution and its products and services. It can also, as many of the universities and polytechnics have identified, be a source of income either through forms of voluntary donation or as direct clients.

Critical to these processes is a continuing dialogue between the segmented markets and the institution through a range of appropriate media such as promotional materials, promotional events and effective 'points of entry' into the institution whether through a telephone switchboard or a reception counter. Given increasing competition between institutions both nationally and internationally these points of contact will need to reflect the expectations of clients for quality services and products. It is however worth stressing that the major source of market information available to institutions are existing and immediately past students. This reinforces the value of student evaluation and feedback, a point discussed in more detail later in this chapter.

In addition to local market intelligence there will be a growing need for institutions to be aware of developments within the European Commission and each member state of the Community. In this area there is a real danger of information overload and the unproductive and indiscriminate distribution of information. Each institution will need to develop strategies by which it makes accessible a wide range of information sources while targeting information received to appropriate individuals and parts of its sub-structure. This does call for a clear information policy for the institution based on information needs analysis and an audit of current information flows. It will need to identify existing and potential sources of information and relate the cost of information acquisition, retrieval and storage against the identified benefit stemming from the information received. There are already a number of reference sources available ranging from European document centres, European information centres, the Central Bureau of the EC, CEDEFOP, and the agencies of central and local government.

Access to contemporary information is a prerequisite for effective curriculum development. The pace of change resulting from the Single European Market and developments in vocational education at EC, national, regional and local levels will make the development of effective market information sources a major priority. However the availability of information identifying the potential market opportunity, does not, and should not, predetermine action by the institution. The nature and extent of such action will need to be based on the operational judgements of managers and staff of the institution informed by a shared awareness of its overarching 'mission' or purpose. This presupposes the existence of a clear institutional 'mission' which informs priority decision-making. These issues will be explored in Chapter 6.

Design of learning programmes

The implications of the Single European Market will significantly intensify current developments in the design of learning programmes. Increasingly programmes will be required to offer that which clients, whether individual or corporate, want and demand. Learning programmes will increasingly represent the product of a design partnership between professional educationalists and clients, packaged to meet specific needs and employing a wide range of teaching and learning strategies, many with little or no recourse to traditional didactic teaching methods. In many cases learning programmes will include pre-determined outcome measures informed by explicit occupational standards. Past experience will be valued and rewarded through mechanisms which accredit prior learning with individual attainment recorded through records of achievement and similar mechanisms.

The economic requirement for a more competent and capable work force will strengthen the notion of educational achievement as an individual right and the concomitant development of an entitlement curriculum within each institution. Variations of an entitlement curriculum are already in operation in some areas for the 16–19 age group through the extension of the Technical Vocational Educational Initiative (TVEI), and it can be seen to underpin both the Enterprise in Higher Education Initiative and a range of other initiatives in higher education sponsored by the Employment Department Training Agency (EDTA, 1989a):

> The workplace of today and tomorrow requires employees who are resourceful and flexible and who can adapt quickly to changes in the nature of their skills and knowledge. They would need to be able to innovate, recognize and create opportunities, work in a team, take risks and respond to challenges, communicate effectively and be computer literate. These attributes are the core skills of an enterprising person and lie at the heart of any enterprising culture.
>
> Enterprise is necessary to running a business and working in industry and commerce but the term embraces a wide spectrum of human endeavour and is needed in a variety of situations and contexts. Enterprise makes for both effective performance in employment and personal fulfilment in a changing world.
>
> The Training Agencies Enterprise in Higher Education Initiative is part of the broader enterprise movement. It has been introduced in order to encourage the development of qualities of enterprise amongst those seeking higher education qualifications. (EDTA, 1989b, p. 4)

As with TVEI, critical to the curriculum development promoted by the Enterprise in Higher Education Initiative is the recognition that enterprise programmes should be fully integrated with existing educational provision and not be 'bolt-on' modules of business studies or economics (this issue is explored by McDonald in this text).

TVEI has also introduced individual profiling, through records of achievement, more fully into further education than before, although this has created problems of overlap with the NCVQ's National Record of Vocational Achievement (NROVA). Given the significance of records of achievement in recording those elements of programmes not currently accredited by existing qualifications it can be anticipated that a single recording mechanism will be introduced by UK central government by 1992. Modularized programmes have been introduced into many areas of higher education linked to the CNAA's credit accumulation and transfer scheme (CNAA, 1989a).

These and other initiatives may be seen as attempts to broaden curriculum opportunities and in the case of the accreditation of prior learning and credit accumulation and transfer schemes, to widen access opportunities. The principle underlying the credit accumulation and transfer scheme (CATS) is that learning, wherever it occurs and providing it can be assessed, should be given credit towards a qualification. This promotes a far greater degree of flexibility of learning opportunities for students than traditionally available. It allows for study to occur on a full- or part-time basis, or by open or distant learning methods, and does not normally penalize breaks in study.

Many higher educational institutions have now established their own CATS schemes, or have done so in partnership with other institutions, using the CNAA's tariff system. The CATS scheme has encouraged many institutions to develop modular programmes of study either across the whole institution or in particular vocational areas where demand for a flexible approach has been identified. Particular areas where this has occurred include: engineering, areas of professional health care, and general management training (CNAA, 1989b).

In 1989 a European Community Course Credit Transfer System (ECTS) was established under the ERASMUS programme for a pilot period of six years to develop systems for recognizing and transferring credit for achievement by study and work in different member states. As with the development of tables of comparability of vocational qualifications, it must be anticipated that credit transfer schemes designed to facilitate opportunities for students to move across national boundaries in pursuit of their education will grow to become an increasingly significant part of the curriculum provision of each institution.

The Single European Market will intensify the existing requirement for a flexible and relevant curriculum. Demands to improve access opportunities for non-traditional groups will call not only for changes in marketing and the breakdown of barriers to access, but also the programming of provision at times of the day, days of the week, and in sequences, which are currently outside the majority of existing practice. It will make more urgent the need to develop flexible access routes and progression opportunities which take full account of each individual's prior experience. At the same time curriculum planners will need to respond to increasing demands for PICKUP-type provision, perhaps most specifically in the area of language training, and decide the extent to which they wish to offer short courses or one-to-one training as part of their total portfolio of provision.

While the marketing and pricing of provision for PICKUP clients will be different from those for non-traditional groups a commitment to quality should exist for both. Equally access to information and communications technologies should be similar, as should concern for developing the appropriate teaching and learning strategies to be employed with experienced adult learners. The development by BTEC and others of 'European units' will support the Europeanization of the curriculum, however it will be for institutions to ensure that these are fully integrated into the curriculum and not 'bolt-on' additions with cosmetic rather than educational value. Combined, these competing factors will make the curriculum design challenge of the 1990s more intense and more challenging than ever before.

Delivering learning programmes

Stanton suggests that:

> ... if needs analysis and curriculum design are done well enough, implementation almost follows of itself. If learners have a full and complete understanding of what they are aiming for and how to recognize when they have got there, then, though they will still require facilities and tutoring, they may not require teaching in the traditional way ... that could become very important when coping with the volume of change resulting from the demographic trends and the diversity of the economy, at the same time as colleges are being required to be more efficient. (Stanton, 1989, p. 24)

To achieve this however teaching and learning strategies need to be developed so as to empower individuals to take ownership of their own learning and develop the level of capability required to respond to the implications of the Single European Market. Certainly the challenge for curriculum designers will be to integrate into learning programmes opportunities for the development of specific competences and more holistic individual capability. Critical to this will be the application of teaching and learning strategies which facilitate and support processes of student reflection, experimentation and evaluation while promoting self-worth and encouraging a propensity for lifelong learning (see for example Kolb, 1984, Boud et al, 1985). There are a range of mechanisms to promote such experiential learning ranging from work and community placements to forms of 'learning by doing' (Gibbs, 1988). All seek to ensure that the individual can 'do' rather than simply 'know' although they differ in emphasis and degree of student ownership.

Exemplary among these forms is the Independent Study initiative originating from the Polytechnic of East London in the 1970s: 'Independent Study is based on the proposition that learners will learn best and develop more as self-respecting, responsible and competent human beings, if in association with others, they take responsibility for the planning and execution of their own learning' (Stephenson, 1986, p. 54). The philosophy of Independent Study is one which emphasizes the learning needs of the learner. It acknowledges that it is the learner who best knows his or her own learning needs and how these might best be met. It further acknowledges that to support and facilitate the learner requires a body of skills and competence among staff, the development and construction of systems of consultation, discussion, negotiation and assessment designed to deliver learning opportunities at the appropriate level and with the necessary rigour.

Central to the Independent Study approach is the construction of a 'learning contract' between the individual and the institution. Once validated the 'learning contract' guarantees a given level of qualification subject to the individual meeting the performance indicators he or she has determined. This process empowers the individual to determine his or her own learning needs, how these can best be met and how achievement and development can best be demonstrated. It does this in an environment which is both supportive yet challenging at different levels of evaluation: self-evaluation, peer evaluation, tutor evaluation and institutional evaluation. While the application of Independent Study is currently limited the use of 'learning contracts' can be identified anecdotally in a number of current developments across the UK. In terms of the degree of student ownership of learning these go beyond the more numerically significant growth of negotiated educational action planning which has formed part of employment training and will be significant in the pilot training credit schemes with the potential of forming part of any formalized post-16 curriculum entitlement. Certainly the learning contract mechanism offers a means of coordinating the learning experience of an individual seeking NVQ accreditation while allowing potential opportunities for the development of capability. It might also provide an effective mechanism to support workplace assessment whether undertaken in the UK or on mainland Europe, and the prior identification of learning areas to be supported through work placements. As such it offers a means of delivering liberal vocationalism and fully integrating a European dimension into the curriculum.

The potential growth in demand for PICKUP-type provision associated with the implications of the Single European Market will need to be met by more explicit use of experiential learning methods. The HMI report, *The Contribution of Further and Higher Education to Professional, Industrial and Commercial Updating*, was critical of the delivery of PICKUP provision:

> ... a quarter of all classes seen fell significantly short of a satisfactory level. Where weaknesses were noted, these were often related to poor management of time, the slow pace of the class, badly produced teaching materials or inappropriate teaching methods. In the least successful classes, there was a lack of expertise in adapting teaching strategies to meet the needs of mature learners and the notion that students

on PICKUP courses required information to be transmitted from teacher to student only by means of lectures or by dictating notes was prevalent. Too often, there was a tendency to ignore students' previous learning and experience. (DES, 1987, p. 4)

Critical to the improvement of quality in PICKUP provision will be the use of teaching and learning strategies which are acceptable to work-experienced adults and which are provided flexibly at times convenient to individual students and employers. As such the implications of the Single European Market may act as a spur to the development of modular and competence-based curricula, and individualized forms of learning. However it must also be recognized that such methods may be new and potentially intimidating to learners, particularly those whose educational experience has been in traditional didactic mode. This emphasizes the need for effective pre-admissions advice and guidance and carefully planned induction as coherent elements of curriculum design.

Many of the same issues apply to the provision of vocational education to non-traditional groups although greater attention may need to be placed on the identification and delivery of support mechanisms appropriate to individual needs. A number of examples of innovative actions to support non-traditional groups have already been identified:

- women returners undertaking college training and international workplace experience in the area of import-export administration in response to a particular labour market need;
- long term unemployed people undertaking college-based training and European based workplace experience to develop clerical and secretarial skills through the creative application of Employment Training monies;
- examples of schemes to access physically and sensorally disabled people on to mainstream educational opportunities so as to encourage and facilitate their academic and career development. (Funnell, 1990, p. 22)

While effective market research and curriculum design will create the basis for an effective curriculum response to the implications of the Single European Market, the success of its delivery will be determined by the teaching and learning strategies employed and the range and quality of support services available to individual students. The need to consider libraries, educational media, open access facilities, advice, guidance and counselling facilities and the range of other support services available in institutions as essential components of the total learning experience is axiomatic. Teaching and learning strategies which give greater ownership of learning to the individual student will result in greater demands being placed on these support services. The effective delivery of learning in response to the implications of the Single European Market will need to acknowledge and respond to this.

In the short term this increased demand is likely to be most acutely felt in areas of information and communications technologies. However given the high capital investment costs of such technologies institutions will need to consider a range of strategies for supporting students in these areas such as 'compact' arrangements with employers and extended forms of commercial sponsorship.

Review and evaluation of learning interactions

The effective delivery of vocational education in response to the implications of the Single European Market will critically depend on the effective evaluation of learning programmes. Since the mid-1980s there has been a significant surge of interest in evaluation and the development of performance indicators to assess efficiency and effectiveness (Müller and Funnell, 1991). More recently attention has turned to the development of quality assurance procedures, specifically British Standard 5750 and its European equivalent ISO 9000, and the development of total quality management systems with their emphasis on 'zero defect'. The tension between these initiatives is significant and is one which institutions will need to address if they are to offer a quality response to the implications of the Single European Market.

Rogers and Badham have suggested that at its best a system of evaluation should serve to:

- identify specific target areas for development;
- indicate the level of achievement sought in relation to specific targets;
- indicate the timescale in which particular outcomes are to be achieved;
- make the evaluation parameters explicit and agreed so that key personnel understand clearly what is required;
- provide reliable data on which to base decisions for forward planning;
- reduce managers' dependence on information which is essentially impressionistic and/or of an ad hoc nature. (Rogers and Badham, 1990, p. 92)

In this view evaluation must be seen as an integrative and coherent component of the institution's cycle of planning, implementation and review, and not an isolated or 'bolt-on' activity. This view is shared by the County of Avon Evaluation Project which argues:

- that evaluation should be treated as an integral and essential element throughout the process of course planning, delivery and review;
- that evaluation is best undertaken by those most closely involved in the delivery of provision – the course team;
- that effective monitoring and evaluation requires a systematic, organized approach (Avon, 1988, p. 1).

Indeed the issues of integration, ownership of the process of evaluation by practitioners, and the systematic organization of evaluation, are consistent themes which run throughout the research literature.

Critical to this process is the developing recognition that course or programme teams should be identified as the primary agents of quality assurance supported by systematic procedures for developing student, employer and peer group evaluation within an overarching supportive management structure. Miller and Dower, reviewing quality assurance in the further education sector, suggest that:

> ... the course team should be seen as a vehicle for monitoring, evaluating and improving quality. The course team has the potential for identifying the questions to ask of the course, whether these be directly factual ... or process-orientated... The course team is potentially a conduit of information to the management of the college but of equal importance, it has the potential for notifying managers and others of the changes which it perceives as necessary for the further improvement of the provision. The course team is not merely an agent for gathering data – it should be a powerful means of making and proposing changes. (Miller and Dower, 1989, p. 14)

Developing their analysis Miller and Dower suggest that:

> The course team in the future could well become accountable, not only for the quality of the learning it provides, but also for the quality of resource, in terms of teachers' time, non-teaching time materials and space, which it utilizes. This means that the course team could become the user of efficiency measures and not simply the provider ... (p. 13)

What emerges from this analysis is that the processes and product of evaluation must be owned by practitioners and that these must fully inform the process of curriculum development and the provision of effective support services.

Clearly many institutions offering vocational education have developed comprehensive systems of course or programme evaluation based on these principles. Indeed the existence of such systems are essential components of the forms of institutional and course accreditation granted by validating bodies such as CNAA and BTEC. Such systems are not however without their practical difficulties. McNay in a comprehensive investigation of further and higher education focuses specifically on the constraints and the contradictions experienced by course leaders and other 'activity managers' in facilitating effective workings of course teams (McNay, 1988). Among these he identifies conflicting tasks and priorities; role and status strains; and insufficient staff development and career progression. Nonetheless this approach to evaluation must be seen as the minimum required by institutions.

It must however be questioned whether this approach to evaluation is sufficient when employed in relation to forms of learning which give ownership of the delivery and assessment of learning to the learner. The tension to be explored is between an approach which seeks to maintain and enhance educational standards, critically associated in vocational education with occupational competence, with the emerging liberal vocationalism which is seeking to develop capability through individualized learning programmes. This is likely to increase both internal and external demands for institutions to move towards total quality management which in practice will mean building quality into the educational process rather than identifying specific evaluative periods when defects are inspected out. Such a process also achieves the major rationale of the 'quality movement' which is to understand and conform to the requirements and needs of customers.

If the product of vocational education is the student him or herself then this does imply a very major role for the student in evaluating his or her vocational education experience. Given the enhanced competition generated by the Single European Market and its impact on the delivery of learning programmes it would seem likely that institutions will need to address pro-actively the development of total quality management systems. If true it will generate a significant management challenge, one explored in more detail in the following chapter.

A curriculum framework for enhanced Europeanized learning opportunities

The preceding analysis suggests the need to develop within institutions a curriculum framework to deliver enhanced Europeanized learning opportunities. Such a framework should be based on a concept of 'value added', one which goes beyond that which is readily quantifiable to a concern with student perceptions of personal growth and development through vocational education and its occupational impact.

A model for a framework of this kind is presented in Figure 2. The model illustrates a series of sequential steps commencing with services delivered at the 'point of entry' into vocational education to support the learner determining a programme of study to meet his or her own needs. This may be delivered in a variety of forms for example: coherent progression guidance from school to further or higher education; NVQ-related student admissions procedures, possibly linked to the accreditation of prior learning (Wirral, 1989); or more sophisticated processes of prior determination of an individual learning contract. In all cases individualized support should encourage learners to take ownership of the learning experience and assess the potential value of that experience in relation to individual goals, whether explicitly vocational or more personal.

A comprehensive programme of induction should support the learner in developing study and investigative skills, and in many cases the confidence, to make full use of the learning and support services available

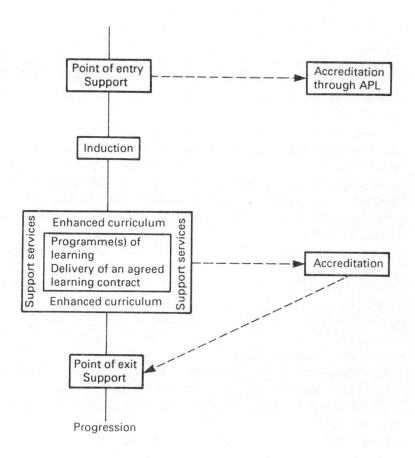

Figure 2 *A curriculum framework for enhanced Europeanized learning opportunities*

in the institution. This needs to go beyond traditional course induction to concern itself with the promotion of a culture which values experimentation and opportunity, openness and tolerance, and responsibility and respect. It is unlikely that this can be achieved without a major initiative at the institutional level and the coordination of such an induction programme by a separate institutional sub-set with responsibility for student affairs – typically the student services unit of a polytechnic or university. The primary function of such an induction should not be socialization, however important this is, but rather the generation of a sense of ownership of the institution by the learner and a recognition of its fundamental facilitative role.

The effective delivery of learner competence and capability will require the enhancement of existing programmes of study to provide breadth, coherence and flexibility in the curriculum. It was suggested earlier that this might best be achieved through an individualized learning contract although both TVEI and the Enterprise in Higher Education Initiative offer examples of good and innovative practice which support the liberal vocationalism required to respond to the implications of the Single European Market.

Finally the model proposes support at the 'point of exit' from vocational education. This might be offered through vocational and educational advance, guidance and counselling both within institutions and through external agencies. Such provision would need to complement, and not duplicate, existing practice particularly that offered by an LEA careers service. Clearly all institutions offer forms of 'point of exit' support with much, if not the majority, being undertaken by course tutors and other members of the lecturing staff with support from a student counsellor or an educational or vocational guidance service. This is, however, unlikely to be sufficient either as a component of a full learner entitlement or as a means of supporting educational progression and fully informed choices in relation to identified areas of skill shortage. Indeed it is unlikely to be sufficient in encouraging learner retention in the increasingly competitive world of vocational education.

As with all other developments expansion of these important support services has resource implications and generates opportunity costs. The implications of the Single European Market both intensify these issues by increasing demand and expectations for such services and also offers a potential solution to resourcing issues through managed cross-subsidization from profit-generating activity.

Curriculum change and enhancement cannot be achieved without significant impact on the institution itself and the human resource therein. These issues are explored in the following two chapters.

References

Bilbrough, B et al (1988) *Developing the Responsive College*, Coombe Lodge Report, vol. 20, no. 10, Further Education Staff College, Blagdon

Boud, D, Keogh, R, Walker, D (eds) (1985) *Reflection: Turning Experience into Learning*, Kogan Page, London

Council for National Academic Awards (1989a) *Background Papers to the CNAA's Credit Accumulation and Transfer Scheme*, CNAA, London

Council for National Academic Awards (1989b) *The Work of the Credit Accumulation and Transfer Scheme* (CATS), CNAA, London

County of Avon (1988) *Evaluation Strategies in NAFE*, County of Avon Evaluation Project, Bulletin 3

Department of Education and Science Report by HM Inspectors (1987) *The Contribution of Further and Higher Education to Professional, Industrial and Commercial Updating,* DES, Stanmore

Employment Department Training Agency (1989a) *Changing Higher Education,* EDTA, Moorfoot

Employment Department Training Agency (1989b) *Enterprise in Higher Education,* EDTA, Moorfoot

Funnell, P (1990) *Staff Development Implications of a Single European Market,* FEU Research Project: RP596, Further Education Unit, London

Further Education Unit (1989) *Towards a Framework for Curriculum Entitlement,* DES, London

Gibbs, G (1988) *Learning by Doing,* Further Education Unit, London

Kerr, J F (ed) (1968) *Changing the Curriculum,* University of London Press, London

Kolb, D A (1984) *Experiential Learning – Experience as the Source of Learning and Development,* Prentice-Hall, New Jersey

McNay, I (1988) *The Reality of College Management,* Longman for the FEU, York

Miller, J and Dower, A (1988) *Coping with crisis: Management development in FHE,* Longman for the FEU, York

Müller, D and Funnell, P (1991) *Delivering Quality in Vocational Education,* Kogan Page, London

Rogers, G and Badham, L (1990) 'Partners in Evaluation', *Education,* 3 August

Stanton, G (1989) 'The Way Forward', *Further Education Promoting Enterprise,* Further Education Unit, London

Stephenson, J (1986) 'Individualism Within Communities: A Way Forward for WEF?', *'New Era' Journal of the World Education Fellowship,* vol. 67, Issue 3

Wirral Metropolitan College (1989) *The Delivery of Competence-based Learning and Achievement,* Bulletin 3, Wirral Metropolitan College and NCVQ

6 Managing Institutional Change

The Education Reform Act 1988 has created major changes in the structure and organizational relationships existing within institutions offering vocational education (see for example Lawton et al, 1989, Betts et al, 1988). Underpinning much of the detail of the Act has been an attempt to give greater freedom of action to institutions either through individual corporate status or greater forms of delegation from the maintaining LEA. Linked with this has been an attempt to introduce new forms of managerialism into the delivery of vocational education designed to combat perceived inefficiencies in the system and a new responsiveness to the changing needs of learners, employers and local communities.

This has promoted a clear recognition of the need for a closer and fuller relationship between industry, commerce and vocational education in the light of the evidence of a 'failure to train' discussed in earlier chapters. The Education Reform Act has generated enormous change within institutions at the levels of organizational structure and process, while confronting the traditional culture of institutions with a new entrepreneurialism based ideologically on the notion of the supremacy of market mechanisms. It is within this organizational context that the implications of the Single European Market will need to be addressed.

Organizational culture

There can be little doubt that the Single European Market will impact significantly on the organizational culture of institutions offering vocational education. Different cultures will predominate in different institutions, and indeed cultural variations may be identified in different subsets of the same institution. As Handy suggests:

> . . . anyone who has spent time within any variety of organizations, or worked in more than two or three, will have been struck by the differing atmospheres, the differing

ways of doing things, the differing levels of energy, of individual freedom, of kinds of personality. For organizations are as different and varied as the nations and societies of the world. They have differing cultures – sets of values and norms and beliefs – reflected in different structures and systems. And the cultures are affected by the events of the past and by the climate of the present, by the technology and the type of work, by their aims and the kind of people which work in them. (Handy, 1985, p. 185)

Handy identifies four models of organizational culture: the power culture (traditionally associated with small entrepreneurial organizations); the role culture (often stereotyped as a bureaucracy); the task culture (associated with matrix organizations being task- or project-centred in its organizational form); the person culture (with the individual at the centre of an organization which is there solely to serve and assist). For Handy the factors influencing an organization's culture, and the structure which flows from this, are: the organization's history and ownership; its size and the technology it employs; its goals and objectives; the external environment, including the competitive nature of its markets; and the people within the organization.

Differentiated cultures with their associated structures and systems may exist in any organization. So for example role cultures may typify those areas of an institution which operate on a relatively routine basis against fixed timescales and a stable external environment. Conversely marketing or curriculum development units of an institution are likely to develop a task-culture which brings people and other resources together to facilitate successful task completion. Such differentiation can be entirely successful if it is fully integrated so as to support the achievement of the overarching 'mission' of the institution and if there is a harmony between each individual in the institution and the particular culture with which he or she interacts. This latter point acknowledges the importance of the psychological contract which develops between an individual and his or her employer and the importance of this in relation to individual job satisfaction and the quality of the contribution the individual makes.

Reflecting on this Handy offers the following hypothesis:

- Individuals with a low tolerance for ambiguity will prefer the tighter role prescriptions of a role culture.
- High needs for security will be better met in the role culture.
- A need to establish one's identity at work will be appropriate in a power or task culture. In a role culture it will be seen as a 'person' orientation and thought disruptive.
- The impact of individual skills and talents will be more marked in power and task cultures than in role. Hence greater care needs to be paid to the selection and appraisal of individuals in these cultures.
- Low calibre people resources ... would push an organization towards a role culture, where jobs can be defined down to the level of manpower available. (Handy, 1985, p. 204)

Within this context cultural diversity is both tolerable and potentially advantageous; however it demands a degree of integration which serves a single corporate mission and which promotes a realization that diversity has been designed to achieve that mission.

As the implications of the Single European Market reinforce change generated by the Education Reform Act, and indeed a range of curriculum and other factors, so the requirement for organizational differentiation will grow with a concomitant need for increasing clarity and employee ownership of the corporate mission. This view is in line with the dictates of total quality management (Müller and Funnell, 1991) and with the findings of Goldsmith and Clutterbuck in their review of the factors influencing organizational success in the industrial and commercial sectors (Goldsmith and Clutterbuck, 1984). However in addition to cultural diversity institutions must anticipate a significant requirement for change in response to the implications of the Single European Market.

It is likely that the requirement for an entrepreneurial response to the implications of the Single European Market will drive institutions towards major structural and procedural changes. It is questionable however whether such changes will be successful without an associated change in the organizational culture of the institution. This begs the question whether an organization's culture can be changed? The evidence offered by Goldsmith and Clutterbuck suggests that it can. On the basis of this evidence they suggest the following guidelines for generating cultural change:

- First, identify the culture you have. . .
- Second, identify what kind of culture best fits the market you operate in. Consider particularly who buys the product and whether cost or quality is the key criterion in the buying decision. . .
- Third, consider what organizational changes have to be made to accommodate any change of culture. . .
- Fourth, consider what personnel changes must be made. The place to start is the top . . . it is of no value for top management to issue edicts if it does not follow them up with continued, and unequivocal and uncontradicted action. Culture changes happen as people observe behaviour and attitudes at work, and stimulate them into their own ways of thinking and doing. (Clutterbuck and Goldsmith, 1984, p. 163)

Critical to the successful development of cultural change is leadership. There has been little research on the significance of institutional leadership in the delivery of vocational education and this may reflect the historic legal power of academic boards and the political control of institutions by elected local authorities. The Education Reform Act, 1988, has significantly changed this position and introduced a greater degree of executive action into the management of institutions. This will place a new emphasis on the significance of leadership in facilitating organizational change within institutions offering vocational education. Indeed it can be strongly argued that while it is through the empowering of individuals that organizations change, the creation of a culture which welcomes, supports and encourages change is a product of effective leadership. Critical to this is the clear articulation of the institutional mission presented as a coherent 'vision' to all members of staff. To quote Hesburgh: 'The very essence of leadership is [that] you have a vision. It's got to be a vision you articulate clearly and forcefully on every occasion. You can't blow an uncertain trumpet' (Hesburgh, 1987).

Such leadership will facilitate individuals and teams to work towards the explicit strategic and operational goals of the institution. It will need to permeate the whole institution and create both a 'love of change' (Peters, 1988) and a high regard for experimentation. Indeed it requires the creation of a learning culture within the institution which mirrors the forms of learning experience it wishes to offer its clients. As such it will support the development of a culture which perceives the role of vocational educational providers as leading and enhancing provision so as to ensure that learners fully participate in the learning process such that they become responsible for creating, delivering and evaluating the product of such provision. Finally and critically it will need to support the development of a culture which is fully European in outlook and which seeks to integrate the European dimension into the curriculum of the 'whole institution'.

Institutional structures and processes

Embedding enhanced Europeanized learning opportunities into an institution requires significant decisions about organizational structures and processes. As discussed in Chapter 3 many institutions have moved towards matrix structures which include organizational units responsible for curriculum or product innovation or aspects of institutional marketing. In all cases these structures demonstrate elements of a task culture and have been put in place to facilitate and enhance the institution's response to changing market circumstances and client demand. An increasing number of institutions have created separate organizational units in the form of a European office, a research and development unit, a marketing or enterprise unit or similar, or an identified individual, to initiate and coordinate European-focused developments.

Linked to these structures have been processes which centralize many aspects of European-focused innovation and contacts, and the analysis and storage of information. Such arrangements have significant advantages. A relatively small-sized organizational unit has the advantage of being task-focused and extremely adaptable. It can be highly responsive to market demands, and highly influential if it has a position in the organizational hierarchy which allows it to report directly to senior management. The centralization and coordination of contacts with partner institutions on mainland Europe or funding bodies such as the EC avoids unproductive duplication, can minimalize the more destructive elements of micro-political competition, and present a coherent corporate image to the external environment. Such arrangements can also tap the entrepreneurial skills of existing members of staff of the institution and thereby offer them job satisfaction and potential career development.

Despite these advantages this approach has two significant weaknesses. First, it can lead to excessive centralism with complex administrative and other procedures which act as a constraint on innovation. It can act as a disincentive to individual members of staff to reflect upon and evaluate the implications of the Single European Market on their professional role and activity, and so constrain the development of a 'whole institutional' approach. Critically it can lead to the Single European Market being 'somebody else's business' with a resultant failure to develop a fully integrated European culture in the institution. As such it can also constrain marketing activity and the production of new and educationally viable learning programmes.

In practice much will depend on the ability of these organizational units to facilitate positive action by others and the sharing of information and good practice if these disadvantages are to be avoided. This does require the prior determination of a statement of purpose for the activity and an explicit understanding by the whole institution of the role and purpose of the unit and its span of activity.

The second potential disadvantage stems in part from the first. At least in its early stages the development of an organizational unit to promote Europeanized learning opportunities is likely to constitute a net additional cost to the institution. In a situation of explicit budgetary restraint this can be perceived by the staff of an institution as having a detrimental impact on the quality of learning for existing students, if only in terms of the opportunity cost of providing the new activity. Such perceptions can lead to cynicism about the activity leading to it being marginalized rather than fully integrated into the institution. This creates its own 'self-fulfilling prophecy' as its marginal status leads to it failing to deliver acceptable forms of innovation, so reinforcing earlier cynicism.

As with other similar initiatives these potential problems can be reduced if the unit has clear and explicit managerial support and access through the institution's academic board or its sub-structures to the appropriate forums of institutional debate. It also stresses the importance of including the European dimension in the mission statement of the institution, and for this to be developed through participative mechanism which will support the statement being owned by all members of staff.

Given full integration into the corporate life of the institution an organizational unit of this kind can play a significant part in enhancing Europeanized learning opportunities. It can play a role in undertaking information audits and needs analysis allowing the targeting of appropriate information to the right part of the institution at the right time to inform decision-making. It can also manage the interface with external bodies whether in the UK or on mainland Europe so as to ensure that curriculum or product development opportunities are taken and that external sources of funding are sought where they will contribute to the curriculum and the learning opportunities offered by the institution. It can also link together existing disparate EC, national and local initiatives to ensure they are managed coherently. It should facilitate the integration of a European dimension informed by the local commercial and industrial context into academic planning procedures and the planning and allocation of capital, equipment and consumables budgets. It can support the integration of initiatives such as the LX network, PICKUP Europe Unit and Regional Technology Centres into a single point of entry for both prospective clients and other members of staff of the institution. It can also be an instigator of short course, consultancy and research provision linking specifically to the needs of local and regional markets.

However its primary role should be the creation of an organizational culture which is supportive of, and responsive to, the enhancement of Europeanized learning opportunities. As such the primary task of such a unit is the creation of a situation in which its contribution becomes largely, if not wholly, redundant as individual tasks and the underpinning European culture becomes fully embedded into the whole institution. To promote this both quantitative and qualitative performance indicators should be developed to monitor and evaluate progress with formal reporting mechanisms through the organizational structure.

In addition to the broad area of curriculum development a range of administrative processes will need to be developed in order to offer a quality response to the implications of the Single European Market. The importance of the 'point of entry' of clients into the institution has already been stressed. The capacity to communicate in multiple languages in both written and spoken forms is likely to become increasingly important. Procedures for supporting exchange visits and work placements will be required together with procedures for the reimbursement of course fees from students from other EC member states. More locally a growth in PICKUP activity and work with non-traditional groups stimulated by the Single European Market will have important implications for the wide range of learner-related administrative procedures currently operating.

In particular enrolment procedures, the purchase of consumables used specifically by learners and procedures concerned with quality assurance will need review.

Finally the currently significant set of planning, professional and resourcing arrangements with external bodies will be intensified by the implications of the Single European Market. Two examples illustrate this point. In all vocational education sectors (and not solely maintained colleges) a relationship with one or more local authorities will be important in promoting education and training associated with economic development. Indeed the interface between large-scale infrastructure development and its associated vocational education needs is an issue of increasing significance given the requirement for Community-wide tendering for major items of public procurement. Equally, developing relationships at the institutional level can be identified with the Employment Department Training Agency. This may prove increasingly significant for securing support for innovative curriculum projects (see Bonney in this text).

Strategic and operational management

Earlier in this chapter emphasis was given to the importance of visible leadership in creating a culture responsive to change. As such a key element of leadership is a capacity to influence and organize meaning for others. Much recent research has distinguished between this notion of leadership and one of management. As an example Bennis and Namus suggest that: 'managers are people who do things right and leaders are people who do the right thing. The difference may be summarized as activities of vision and judgement – effectiveness versus activities of mastering routine-efficiency' (Bennis and Namus, 1985, p. 44).

The challenge for strategic and operational managers in institutions offering vocational education is that they are required to be both effective leaders and efficient managers. This not untypical requirement is uniquely complicated by the role of governing bodies, and in the maintained sector by that of LEAs, in determining the strategic direction of the institution and the operational and activity management tasks to be undertaken by designated managers. What exists currently is a tension between the traditions of public sector management and the 'new managerialism' introduced most explicitly by the Education Reform Act. This represents a tension between the traditional management of a 'steady state' bureaucracy and the developing 'business' of vocational education.

This 'new managerialism' offers real opportunities to promote the quality of vocational education while maintaining a genuine commitment to the broader educational principles of access and progression. However there is a real danger that the entrepreneurialism this requires will be constrained by performance indicators which concentrate on quantifiable inputs and outputs of vocational education and not take full regard of the centrality of the learner in the process and his or her qualitative evaluation of the value of the process. This point has been recognized in research undertaken by Haffenden and Brown in the further education sector:

> The impression given by activity managers was that many of the concerns of those with overall financial responsibility were with developing management information systems which could generate the type of performance indicators mentioned in the Joint Efficiency Study. Many of these indicators were looking backwards to an FE of five or more years ago. Indicators like staff:student ratios, average class size and exam pass rates will be very clumsy, if not inappropriate, in dealing with the type of FE system required of the 1990s. (Haffenden and Brown, 1989, p. 13)

This need not however be the case. The application of total quality management approaches in institutions may lead to a greater concern for the needs of the individual learner simply because this is in line with the customer-centred yet entrepreneurial nature of the approach. Indeed there are marked similarities between the attempts to empower the learner through mechanisms such as learning contracts and training credits, and the notions of employee empowerment explicit in total quality management and other new forms of management thinking (see for example Crosby, 1989). Indeed in both cases a critical concern is with the capability of the individual, whether as a learner or as an employee rather than narrow competence. The implications of the Single European Market will create a substantial market-led demand for vocational education which reinforce and stimulate this developing harmony.

During the 1990s the challenge of Europe will grow and intensify. While it will be governing bodies, and LEAs (although the latter is likely to have diminishing significance throughout the 1990s), which provide the strategic steer, it will be for institutional managers to create the structures and procedures to promote an entrepreneurial response to the challenge of Europe. Further it will be for institutional managers to exercise the leadership flair to create the required organizational culture for change in a turbulent environment. These constitute major tasks. It is likely to prove to be an imperative both for institutions themselves and for the economy as a whole that these tasks are met.

References

Bennis, W and Namus, B (1985) *Leaders*, Harper and Row, London

Betts, D et al (1988) *Life after the Education Reform Act*, Coombe Lodge Report vol. 20, no. 11, Further Education Staff College, Blagdon

Crosby, P B (1989) *Lets Talk Quality*, McGraw Hill, London

Goldsmith, W and Clutterbuck, D (1984) *The Winning Streak*, Weidenfield and Nicolson, London

Haffenden, I and Brown, A (1989) *Implications of Competence-Based Curricula*, DES, London

Handy, C (1985) *Understanding Organisations*, Penguin, Middlesex

Hesburgh, T (1987) quoted in T. Peters (1987) *Thriving on Chaos: Handbook for a Management revolution*, Macmillan, London

Lawton, D (ed) (1989) *The Education Reform Act: Choice and Control*, Hodder and Stoughton, London

Müller, D and Funnell, P (1991) *Delivering Quality in Vocational Education*, Kogan Page, London

Peters, T (1987) *Thriving on Chaos: Handbook for a Management Revolution*, Macmillan, London

7 Promoting Human Resource Development

The rationale for a human resource policy

Delivering the curriculum and institutional developments necessary to offer a quality response to the implications of the Single European Market has generated, and will continue to generate, the requirement for human resource development. In order to achieve its aim of enhancing Europeanized learning opportunities, an institution will be required both to maintain and increase the quality and range of provision offered to clients. Success in achieving this will be largely dependent upon the availability of a competent and qualified work-force who are effectively deployed and managed, and who are motivated and committed to achieve the overall mission of the institution. This will require each institution developing a human resource policy and complementary set of strategies designed to: attract and retain staff; promote greater productivity; improve the quality of performance of individuals; contain, and where appropriate reduce, overall staffing costs; and critically improve the flexibility and versatility of staff through an organizational culture which supports an explicit 'love of change'.

The starting point for such developments should be a comprehensive review of the institution's existing human resource policy, focusing critically on: recruitment; reward and retention packages; and staff development and training. This is likely to be most effective if undertaken within a wider context of review, particularly that concerned with curriculum audit and review, and the evaluation of institutional structures, procedures and styles.

The changing practice of vocational education in the 1990s will require that this human resource policy is explicit and understood by staff. The implications of the Single European Market will intensify this requirement at two interacting levels. First, it will change the pattern of demand for vocational education such that it will require greater levels of flexibility from all staff members whether academic, administrative, clerical, technical, or manual employees. At a minimum this will be a consequence of the changing nature of learning programmes, teaching and learning strategies, and new patterns of client demand for short course, consultancy, research and other 'non-standard' forms of provision.

A successful response to this changing demand pattern will require new forms and enhanced levels of flexibility among and between individual members of staff. It will increasingly question the viability of the 'three-term academic year' and a range of other traditional practices. The consequential implications of these developments, for both conditions of service and staff development, are significant. Failure to resolve these issues may act as a constraint on the realization of the required flexibility as might the piecemeal nature of human resource management in institutions. This has been exposed by East in an important FEU discussions document (FEU, 1987). In the foreword to the document Mansell suggests:

> One result of this deficiency in the management of what can be regarded as a large service industry is the persistent isolation of teachers within their own subject expertise. They, and their non-teaching colleagues, are not encouraged to see themselves as members of an organization with corporate aims related to serving the community. Thus, issues such as appraisal, overtime, initial training and continuing professional development, flexible learning, promotion, non-teaching duties, assessment – and so on – are inferably treated as separate from each other, and rarely perceived as being components of what should be a comprehensive personnel function. (p. v)

The foreword goes on to suggest that:

> ... there can be little doubt that while teachers' roles and effectiveness remain anchored in class-contact time and classroom performance, other curricula processes will remain marginalized. Responsiveness, innovation and evaluation will take second place. To release the latent talents of educational staff, a supportive and modern personnel policy is required... (p. vi)

A second level of impact results from individual directives arising from the Single European Act 1987 and associated legislation, most significantly the Community Charter of Fundamental Social Rights (The Social Charter) adopted by eleven of the twelve member states at the Strasbourg European Council meeting in December 1989 – the UK being the exception (CEC, 1989).

Three examples illustrate this point. The directive on the mutual recognition of diplomas discussed in Chapter 4 will create a more intensive market for qualified lecturers in shortage areas across EC boundaries, so exacerbating existing areas of shortage within UK institutions. This may only partly be ameliorated by recruitment from other EC member states. However, where 'staff from other EC countries are recruited, trainers will need to design induction training and other forms of support which are sensitive to cultural differences, in order to facilitate the integration of such staff into the work-force' (Lawes, 1990, p. 36). Further the mutual recognition of professional qualifications will require institutional managers to have access to relevant information about the nature and status of such qualifications if they are to make optimal recruitment decisions. Information of this kind might best be centralized in a discrete personnel function although this does not imply that the control, as opposed to support, of recruitment decisions should be located within this function.

The Social Charter will significantly extend the employment rights of individual workers. Proposals include the right to employee consultation and participation and, of particular importance to institutions offering vocational education, the extension of full-time employment rights to 'atypical' workers such as those on part-time or temporary contracts. Given the traditional reliance of institutions on part-time academic staff, and support staff on temporary contracts, this could generate major net additional costs to institutions. However the value of enhancing the employment conditions of these valuable staff members should not be underestimated, particularly given the inherent flexibility associated with these contractual arrangements, the poor pattern of reward and support traditionally available to these colleagues, and the contribution they make to service provision.

A third and final example relates to the area of health and safety. To quote Lawes:

> UK legislation on health and safety has tended to develop in parallel with EC initiatives. Such legislation produces training needs of itself, but the EC's Framework Directive includes a specific requirement (article 12) that employers provide adequate health and safety training. This directive is part of a proposed package with five subsidiary directives covering: the workplace; the use of machinery, equipment and installations; the use of personal protective equipment; work with VDUs; and handling heavy loads. Training will obviously need to cover both new and existing staff. (Lawes, 1990, p. 36)

Strategies for action

It has been suggested that the implications of the Single European Market will intensify the need for a flexible, competent and qualified work-force capable of responding to a changing European market for vocational education. This will require the development within each institution of a coherent and comprehensive human resource policy.

One aspect of such a policy would need to be a set of recruitment strategies which focus on the developmental potential of individual applicants. This will encourage the appointment of staff on the basis of an assessment of likely contribution over the medium and long term rather than purely in relation to her or his ability to meet short-term operational needs. It will also require reward and retention packages linked to individual performance against explicit criteria and which includes an open and honest process of appraisal.

While potentially contentious, appraisal can facilitate individuals maximizing their own potential while focusing effort on meeting the institutional mission. To quote Wilson discussing teacher appraisal in the context of compulsory education:

> ACAS's definition of appraisal is that it is 'not a series of perfunctory periodic events, but a continuous and systematic process intended to help individual teachers with their professional development and career planning, and to help ensure that the in-service training and deployment of teachers matches the complementary needs of individual teachers and the school'. It relates to induction of probationers, access to in-service training, career management, guidance, counselling and training for teachers experiencing performance difficulty, and reference writing in connection with staff appointments. (Wilson, 1988, p. 99)

Similar supportive mechanisms can be introduced through staff development discussions or similar interview arrangements between a line manager and his or her subordinates. However such arrangements are unable to reward excellent individual action and may as such be of limited value.

There exists, to differing degrees but within all areas of vocational education, a resistance to appraisal. This is understandable where appraisal is perceived as either a form of disciplinary action or where the appraiser is seen by the appraised to be insufficiently competent to undertake the task. The latter may represent an attitudinal resistance to change which may be subject to amelioration on either side through staff development. The former may constitute a legitimate function of appraisal; however, this should not be its primary purpose – indeed it may be seen to have failed if it is only employed in this way. To be effective, appraisal must be a positive and supportive element of the human resource policy and practice of an institution:

> Appraisal ... is a means of identifying development needs. It provides a formal opportunity for the manager's assessment of the year's work to be established and discussed with the member of staff, together with an opportunity for the future year's work to be considered. It also forces reluctant managers to appraise the work of their staff ... [There is no] substitute for the proper accounting by managers for the performance of their staff. Staff need to know where they stand, and managers are

ultimately accountable to their governing bodies and to the taxpayer, and, possibly most importantly, to those they teach. (FEU, 1987, p. 7)

With appraisal defined as a developmental process the apparent tension between it and the notion of employee empowerment discussed in Chapter 6 may be seen to be unfounded. Effective appraisal creates the forum for the review and adjustment of the boundaries within which an individual works, and the resources available to undertake that work. It supports the creative process of matching individual and institutional goals. This approach does however clash with a view which sees the lecturer as sovereign within the classroom, and dominant in a relationship with one or more learners to which no other person has a 'right' of access. Such a view is clearly at variance with the philosophy of liberal vocationalism which places the learner at the heart of the learning process. Indeed the implementation of a liberal vocationalism requires that learner evaluation be a significant element in the appraisal process (Boud, 1990).

Certainly the mechanisms designed to support appraisal must respect the culture of the institution and offer a number of complementary forms – self, peer, student, manager – these being coordinated at a regular and formally recorded meeting with the appraiser. The outcomes of such a process could then be linked to reward through mechanisms such as merit awards or flexible incremental scales. Certainly the linking of reward to actual performance may act as an extrinsic motivator. However it is likely to be more effective when combined with forms of intrinsic reward which include active support and encouragement from a line manager. This latter point reaffirms the importance of effective and visible leadership and the importance of a culture which is both responsive to change and supportive of innovation and experimentation.

The deliberate focus on the individual in this model can facilitate high quality institutional outcomes if it is supported by human resource planning which is both responsive to market needs and based on a prior audit of the skills and competences of current staff. As the implications of the Single European Market encourage institutions to gear up their pace of change, so the requirement both to 'know the staff' and plan progression and succession routes will become increasingly important. Indeed as competition for competent and qualified staff increases so the requirement to design reward packages which support the retention of staff will grow. This needs to be put alongside the requirement to make full use of the staff resource through sensitive amendments to conditions of service. In this sense the implications of the Single European Market will act as one drive towards differentiated patterns of working which acknowledge the requirements and wishes of individual members of staff and facilitate service flexibility by creating patterns of work which acknowledge and respect them. The development of 'management spine' posts in the LEA maintained sector may offer an opportunity for the negotiated introduction of such flexibility within a clear set of contractual conditions.

Increasingly it can be predicted that new forms of employment will emerge which offer a targeted response to particular market demands. As an example a growth in recruitment to technician and demonstrator posts might be predicted in a range of craft, design and technology areas, as cost-effective and flexible forms of employment with significant advantages over traditional academic posts. Equally the developing forms of entrepreneurialism currently visible in all institutions might be expected to grow with employment patterns emerging in response to the need to recruit and retain people able to design and market new forms of provision. The greater powers available to all institutions in the public sector resulting from the Education Reform Act and associated DES circulars (whether or not they hold corporate status) should facilitate this. Certainly it should support both more sophisticated human resource planning linked to other forms of institutional planning activity, and more explicitly localized industrial relations activity.

It must however be recognized that the nature and pace of change may be uncomfortable for many currently employed in vocational education. Any effective set of human resource strategies will need to address this issue through a mix of actions to include: staff development and retraining; redeployment, job rotation and task-specific secondments; and career and personal counselling. It is essential that an institution demonstrates the same commitment to caring for its staff as its students. This must go beyond a pragmatic attempt to maintain industrial relations harmony to demonstrate through planned action a genuine recognition of the value of the individual and the contribution he or she can make, given that the extent of this is ultimately constrained by available resources.

There remains however a potentially inefficient conflict between an emphasis on human resource planning which may generate increasingly rational forms of organizational activity and the entrepreneurialism required to respond quickly to new market demands. To avoid this both the organizational structures of the institution and the attitudes and practices of staff will need to be developed to ensure that pro-active entrepreneurialism can occur within clear institutional strategies, and that individual action is facilitated, and not unnecessarily constrained, by structures and processes. This constitutes a major task for institutional management.

Individual-led staff development

Critical to this whole process will be the development of a wide-ranging and effective staff development programme designed to support and encourage curriculum and institutional developments. There can be little doubt that an institutional response to the implications of the Single European Market which fails to incorporate a staff development pro-gramme will be unsuccessful in the longer term despite the entrepreneur-ial activities of individuals. Specifically such a response is unlikely to benefit from the considered views of senior managers or permeate the whole institution. As such it would run the risk of being marginalized, particularly in situations of higher staff turnover. The provision of a staff development programme will facilitate the development of a 'whole institutional' approach to the Single European Market and contribute to the shared ownership of the institution's mission.

In seeking to respond to the implications of the Single European Market a staff development programme will need to identify and work to meet the needs of each member of staff through the appropriate opportunities and support services:

> This demands a process of initial needs analysis based on the current and predicted future roles and tasks of the individual and the curriculum and managerial priorities of the institution. Needs analysis and subsequent planning will be most effective if it occurs:
> - at the level of the individual through mechanisms such as staff development interviews supported by self-profiling;
> - at the level of course or task teams through the application of quality circles, task exercises or experiential learning approaches;
> - at the level of the institution by the implementation of corporate policy.
>
> It also demands that the staff development undertaken is subsequently evaluated to judge whether it has been effective in meeting identified needs. Ultimately such evaluation should also contribute to the identification of future staff development needs. (Funnell, 1990, p. 24)

In his review of the staff development implications of a Single European Market, Funnell suggests that:

> Given the significance and immediacy of the implications of the Single European Market it will be essential that the staff development strategy adopted by each institution has two dimensions:
> - a focus on staff development for managers with responsibility for strategic policy and planning and the facilitation of curriculum development;
> - a 'whole college' approach which promotes awareness and the development of appropriate skills and competences amongst all staff.
>
> The former is essential in assuring that the implications of the Single European Market are fully recognized in the strategic decisions of the institution... The second acknowledges that the implications of the Single European Market will permeate the whole institution. It must therefore be assumed that all groups of staff will need to

develop new skills and competences whether as a consequence of: curriculum development; responding to the needs of new UK client groups; offering effective 'point of entry' and customer care services to clients from mainland Europe; or responding to technical and other standards associated with the Single European Market . . . equally important is likely to be the development of entrepreneurial skills amongst staff to facilitate a pro-active response to the new educational and training opportunities created. . . (p. 25)

This essentially institution-led model requires that staff development move quickly from a process of initial awareness raising, to needs analysis and the development of new competences which are subsequently applied and evaluated. This approach also stresses the importance of an initial assessment of the skills and competences being sought and the role and current tasks of each individual. Equally it promotes the need for a staff audit to reveal opportunities for staff support and mentoring arrangements between colleagues.

A potential danger however exists with this model. This concerns the ownership of the responsibility for staff development. While the importance of institution-led staff development is not denied there may be a limit to the extent to which individual staff members can be managed without their taking appropriate responsibility for their own development. To quote Müller: 'if education is aimed at teaching people to learn for themselves, should staff development not have the same end?' (Müller, 1988, p. 103).

For Müller the devolving of responsibility for staff development to individuals within educational institutions will support the development of:

. . . an educational organization which has been able to take steps to respond to external pressures through putting the onus of responsibility on individuals. It should be self-evident that an educational institution, in which its staff members are not seeking educational opportunities of this kind for themselves, is clearly incapable of delivering education to others. (p. 106)

This view is in line with the principles of liberal vocationalism and with the development of teaching and learning styles which give the ownership of learning to the individual learner. Earlier it was argued that such an approach encourages the development of both competence and capability and supports a pro-active approach to the implications of the Single European Market. Individual ownership and responsibility for staff development within a supportive organization can promote innovation, a recognition of the contribution each individual makes to meeting institutional goals and a positive attitude toward continuing development. Indeed it is supportive of the current promotion of the value of continuing professional development (see for example FEU, 1989) and in line with the advice of the Institute of Personnel Management (IPM, 1990).

This approach transposes educational ideas into the practice of organizational management and empowers the individual to reflect upon her or his own strengths and weaknesses and construct strategies to respond to them irrespective of that person's position within the organization. So for example a course leader may identify a need to develop curriculum design skills to support the Europeanization of a particular learning programme, while a receptionist may identify a need to develop customer care skills linked to an elementary command of a second Community language.

As such this empowerment offers a model of good practice for curriculum development and is in sympathy with the ideas of total quality management. And just as total quality management makes quality 'everybody's business' so this form of developmental practice encourages both individuals and institutions to recognize that the success of any organization depends on its people. It is therefore truly entrepreneurial in its promotion of experimentation while allowing the sensitive focusing of individual effort towards meeting the institutional mission.

A blueprint for human resource development

For Peters, people in organizations 'must become the primary source of value added, not a "factor of production" to be optimized, minimized and/or eliminated' (Peters, 1987, p. 282). He identifies a number of 'prescriptions' for achieving a flexible, adaptive and responsive organization by empowering people, critically that:

- there is no limit to what the average person can achieve if thoroughly involved;
- the powers of individuals can be most effectively gathered when they are grouped into self-managing teams.

He goes on to suggest that success in achieving organizational and individual flexibility is most likely in situations where:

- there are consistent opportunities for people to be listened to and where achievement is recognized;
- substantial managerial effort is given to recruitment, focusing specifically on desired values and qualities;
- emphasis is given to constant skills upgrading;
- incentive pay based on performance is available to everyone;
- there is an employment guarantee for the major part of the work-force assuming acceptable individual performance;
- structures and supervisory levels have been rationalized;
- the role of middle managers have been changed 'from cop and

guardian of functional fiefdoms to basher of barriers between functions in order to induce true autonomy and speed action-taking at the front line' (p. 282);

- unnecessary procedures and dispiriting working conditions have been removed.

Within the limitations of the model the work of Peters might be seen to offer a useful blueprint for human development in institutions of vocational education. The imperative within this approach is the implementation of the total package of 'prescriptions' together as part of a coherent strategy rather than in an incremental or piecemeal way. This recognizes the likely resistance to change exhibited by organizations and the trepidation individuals might experience when first offered greater opportunities for self-determination in the workplace. Nonetheless the development of a human resource policy based on a notion of employee empowerment within the context of a clear institutional mission represents a major component of a successful response to the implications of the Single European Market.

References

Boud, D (1990) 'Design for Learning Systems' in B Farmer et al *Making Learning Systems Work*, AETT XXIII, Kogan Page, London

Commission of the European Communities (1989) *Communication from the Commission concerning its action programme relating to the Community Charter of Basic Social Rights for Workers*, COM (89) 658, London

Funnell, P (1990) *Staff Development implications of a Single European Market*, FEU Research Project: RP596, Further Education Unit, London

Further Education Unit (1987) *The Personnel Function in Further and Higher Education*, FEU, London

Further Education Unit (1989) *Continuing Professional Development: Towards a National Strategy*, FEU, London

Institute of Personnel Management (1990) *Continuous Development: People and Work*, IPM, London

Lawes, R (1990) 'Preparing the HR Function for the Single European Market', *Training and Development*, April 1990

Müller, D (1988) 'Staff Development: whose responsibility?', *Programmed Learning Education and Training*, 25, 101–106

Peters, T (1987) *Thriving on Chaos: Handbook for a Management Revolution*, Macmillan, London

Wilson, J (1988) *Appraising Teaching Quality*, Hodder and Stoughton, London

PART III

Responding to the Challenge – Five Case Studies

Introduction

The following chapters offer five case studies which illustrate and amplify issues raised in the preceding chapters. The case studies have been written by practitioners who are themselves developing curriculum and product responses to the implications of the Single European Market. Each of the case studies is 'live' and constitutes a particular form of innovative action. Equally each is representative of the wider range of developments occurring in the field. Consequently they range from discussion of a specific course development within a major polytechnic to a brief sketch of the development of an international partnership within the agricultural sector; from a discrete area of professional practice to a discussion of the work of a local educational authority research and implementation team, and to the innovative work of the Workers' Educational Association in the vocational education of trade unionists.

In Chapter 8 McDonald offers a review of the process of curriculum development undertaken to produce a BA (Hons) Business in Europe degree at Manchester Polytechnic. The starting point for the curriculum development team was an institutional policy for Europeanization which encouraged market research and subsequent curriculum design and development to meet a particular need. In this example links with EC partner institutions, and periods of international placements for students, flow from the curriculum and are now a 'bolt-on' consequence of the availability of external resources.

Many of the issues explored by McDonald are taken up by Bonney. He outlines in Chapter 9 the findings of the Cambridgeshire 1992 Project and discusses how these have influenced practical actions taken within the five further education colleges within the County. Critical to Bonney's analysis is the formation of networks whether at national level, through the PICKUP Europe Unit or some other structure, or the local level between individual colleges and between colleges and the LEA. The tension between the principle of collaboration explicit in network arrangements and the new competitive and entrepreneurial culture in vocational education, developing particularly following the Education Reform Act (1988), is acknowledged but not seen as problematic at this time.

This view perhaps reflects the unique characteristics of the Cambridgeshire Project and different findings might be found elsewhere. Certainly the tension between historical patterns of collaboration, and the service ethic which underpin them, and the developing entrepreneurialism of vocational education is likely to grow more intense in areas of market demand associated with the Single European Market. Given their differential status this tension is also likely to be felt more explicitly by institutions within the LEA-maintained sector than those institutions with corporate status, and others such as private trainers, who have greater potential for self-determination.

In their contribution Bemrose and Dobson tease out the curriculum implications of the harmonization of professional qualifications in the area of radiographic education in a context of both specific changes in this field and more general changes in the delivery and design of vocational education. The need to understand more about the educational experiences underpinning professional practice in other member states is strongly argued. Bemrose and Dobson see an urgent need for the design of specific provision to support practitioners from mainland Europe whose previous education and experience does not fully satisfy UK professional bodies. These issues will be common both across the professions and member states; however their intensity will be unique to each profession and state.

In Chapter 11 Doyle discusses the measures undertaken by the Workers' Educational Association to offer trade unionists effective vocational education linked to the implications of the Single European Market. The approach adopted is through partnership arrangements with 'sister' organizations on mainland Europe. The development of language competence is seen as an important component of the WEA's initial activity with a search for external funding again flowing from a strategy to enhance Europeanized learning opportunities.

The value of international partnerships is explored by Drew in Chapter 12. In this case the context is vocational education associated with the agricultural sector. Drew stresses the importance of a European vision, clear institutional priorities and personal contacts as the keys to effective transnational working. The importance of senior managerial commitment to European working, a point touched on by other commentators, is also stressed.

Each case study reveals an overarching commitment to enhancing the curriculum available to students while acknowledging the institutional and human resource implications of such enhancements. Collectively they typify the work being undertaken in many institutions responding to the implications of the Single European Market. Inevitably in answering some questions they raise many more. As such they contribute to the continuing dialogue within and between institutions necessary to ensure the UK makes an effective response to the challenge of Europe.

8 Developing a Curriculum Response: the BA (Hons) Business in Europe Degree at Manchester Polytechnic

Frank McDonald

History

The study of Europe has a long history at Manchester Polytechnic. As one example, a modern languages degree has been running at the Polytechnic for more than 12 years. Additionally a European Studies component has run in the BSc Combined Studies degree since 1982. The BA Business Studies degree at the Polytechnic has for many years offered the option of foreign language study with the possibility of a placement period in a continental company. As a consequence of these curriculum initiatives a core group of staff have developed knowledge and expertise over a wide range of subject areas relating to the study of Europe.

Events within the European Community during the mid-1980s suggested that integration in Europe was entering a new, more dynamic phase, and during this period the Polytechnic became concerned to enhance the Europeanization of all its courses. The strategy that developed was based on the view that the environment in which most students would ultimately work will become increasingly European and that therefore there is a need to include in courses of study, material relevant to the emerging environment. Consequently a Polytechnic policy on Europeanization was developed. The main thrust of this policy was to ask all course committees to investigate the structure of their courses so as to assess the extent to which relevant material or new European issues were included in their curriculum. The policy also sought to provide, wherever possible, opportunities for students to undertake language study and periods of study and/or placement on the continent.

Within the context of the Polytechnic policy the department of economics became convinced that there was a labour market need for graduates who could understand the European business environment and who were trained in language and business skills useful for companies conducting business in existing and emerging European markets. Initial discussions were held with employers who confirmed this view and indicated a demand for such graduates. They also confirmed the view that while there was an array of existing courses which included European and business elements there was no single course available which provided an appropriate package to meet the needs of employers and those of prospective students. The existing courses also lacked sufficient experience of studying and working in other European countries.

Following a period of review the department concluded that a new degree should be launched. This degree would incorporate, utilize and extend existing expertise and knowledge of staff, and construct a package which would meet expected needs. The basic objectives of the degree would be to focus on the European business environment and to integrate the determinants of this environment with the linguistic and business skills necessary to understand and operate in the emerging European economic space. There was also to be close collaboration with continental European institutions of higher education. This was to extend the European experience of students and staff and to be part of a process towards mutually accredited European qualifications.

Deciding the method of development

Two possible routes to developing a degree were identified: a 'bolt-on' approach, and an integrated approach. The 'bolt-on' approach would involve taking units from existing degrees and bolting them together into a core of language and business studies. The integrated approach would require the development of specially constructed units which were European in content. This would involve a new set of core compulsory units necessary to providing a programme of study which would enable basic course objectives to be met.

A 'bolt-on' approach was seen initially to have several advantages, particularly as it would allow for existing expertise and knowledge to be utilized with a minimum of fuss. However there were clear disadvantages with this approach. One of the most significant of these would be the construction of the core that links the 'bolt-on' units into a coherent package. This core would need to ensure that no major requirements of the course was omitted and as such was perceived to require considerable development resources. This was seen to negate the cost-saving value of the approach. It was also apparent that the existing business environment and business techniques units taught in the department were not sufficiently Europeanized and existing language units were too literature-based. Consequently a 'bolt-on' approach would require the construction of a European theme which could be woven into the curriculum either by using special assignments or creating special units of study. Language units would have to be new and concentrate on linguistic skills relevant to students undertaking substantial periods of study on the continent and as a basis for a future career. Within this context it became apparent that the 'bolt-on' approach would not be suitable for the development of the new degree. Consequently, and at a very early stage in the development process, an integrated approach was adopted.

A team of staff who were already heavily committed to teaching European studies began to meet to discuss the philosophy of the new degree. At the same time discussions were begun with colleagues on the role of languages in the scheme. Discussions were also held on how the scheme should be linked with other European institutions of higher education. All of these factors were seen to be inter-related; however the overall philosophy of the degree had to be fixed before questions about the role of languages and placements in educational establishments on the Continent could be answered.

The course philosophy

During early course development discussions three main issues had to be resolved: the area of study (ie what is meant by Europe); whether the aim was to produce specialist or generalist graduates; the balance between the study of the business environment and business techniques.

Generally there is a tendency to equate the European Community (EC) with Europe. While the course development team was aware of the dangers of this approach it seemed clear that the EC is the engine for creating the new European business environment. It is EC legislation and policies which are creating the framework for the existing and emerging European markets and the rest of Europe is strongly influenced by this legislative and policy framework. A decision was made consequently by the course development team to centre the study of Europe on the EC, in particular to provide a sounder understanding of the political and economic forces which operate in and through the institutions of the EC. The team was also aware that many differences and similarities existed among the countries of Europe. A principal was developed that all units on the business environment and business techniques areas should highlight emerging European-wide tendencies together with major differences and similarities between European countries.

It was also recognized that the large economies of the EC tend to dominate the European business environment and it was consequently agreed that the comparative studies elements of the course would be designed to centre on these. However sufficient material would also be provided to all students so as to have the basic expertise to analyse most national markets within Europe.

As the course development team's discussions with potential employers continued a problem emerged concerning the sort of graduate being sought. As a rule the banks wanted material in the programme suitable for graduates to become bankers, accounting and auditing firms were seeking graduates who could become accountants, and so on. It appeared that ideally each potential employer would like programmes suited to their own particular needs. While the course development team was not opposed to the degree being vocational, the idea of it being a training programme for specific occupations was rejected.

In the first instance this was because of limited resources. It may have been possible to provide a degree programme for people to work in, for example, financial services or marketing, but not for a whole range of specific occupations. Also the Polytechnic policy on Europeanization would encourage existing vocational degrees (eg retail, marketing, accounting and finance) to construct programmes which included relevant European material. It therefore seemed pointless to reproduce this in the new degree programme. Secondly, if the programme was too specific it would not provide a well-rounded graduate, knowledgeable about the European business environment and of the business techniques necessary to examine and tackle issues connected to this environment. The objective was to produce graduates who could quickly adapt to training in a host of business operations in the European arena. The course focus was thereby determined based on providing a strong transferable skills base which employing companies could utilize for their own particular needs. In short the course development team was of the view that staff were not trainers but educators. The course aim was to produce people who could be quickly trained by future employers into specific operational tasks.

The decision on the balance between the study of the business environment and business techniques was greatly eased by the course development team's decision to provide well-rounded graduates. Given the poor level of knowledge of the rest of Europe which prevails in the UK the course development team felt it was important to provide units which would expand the knowledge of students about the economic, political, legal and social determinates of the European business environment. This was to be provided in a set of first-year units and a range of options which would allow students to develop special interests.

Long discussions were held over the key business techniques which should be taught. Eventually accounting, finance, marketing, business use of IT, human resource management and business organization were deemed to be important areas of study. With the exception of the latter two all of these areas were included in a core set of units, and some had options whereby students could expand their knowledge in chosen areas.

Finding space within the programme for all the necessary units was however a major problem. The course development team recognized that its members were not strong (at least in a European sense) in the areas of human resource management and business organization. Although elements of these areas were included in some of the proposed units they were not a strong feature. Consequently the course development team decided to investigate the possibility of students gaining greater levels of understanding in these fields during the period of study on the mainland.

The issue of business skills proved to be a contentious area within the course development team. All agreed on the need to build up skills in teamwork, presentational and communications skills. Expertise in analysing and providing potential solutions to real life business problems was also deemed important. Some believed these should be taught in special units. The majority however felt such skills should be developed through assessed work assignments, thereby fully integrating them into the course of study. Therefore it was decided that in assessing work assignments high priority was to be given to developing such skills. Assessed work would involve the use of IT in preparing and presenting work. Often students would work in teams in preparing and presenting their assignments. In many units real world business problems would be used. As the Polytechnic is part of the Training Agency-funded Enterprise Initiative it is anticipated that developments arising through this initiative will provide gateways into 'live' projects.

At this stage in the development programme the course development team was reasonably confident that a basic philosophy had been satisfactorily worked out and that the team was in a position to settle the language and foreign placement components of the new degree.

The language requirement and placement on the mainland

Language units were to be developed to meet two basic requirements: to provide students with language skills in a major EC language so as to allow them to be able to operate in a business setting; and to provide students with sufficient language skills to allow them to study for a significant period of time on mainland Europe.

To facilitate this it was agreed that language teaching would need to occupy approximately 20 per cent of available teaching time and that the course would recruit only post-'A' level language students. A learning programme was developed which placed emphasis on the skills necessary to study academic subjects in a foreign language and the acquisition of language skills necessary for conducting business in that language. Initially the languages offered would be French and German. In the long term the course development team hoped to expand this to include Spanish and Italian; however, this will require some time in order to develop internal language resources and to recruit sufficient students willing and able to tackle them. It was also clear to the course development team that forging links with French and German partners would be less difficult than linking with Spanish and Italian institutions.

During initial research and visits the course development team discovered three higher educational institutions who were very interested in the new degree programme – the Fachhochschule Bochum, the Université de Savoie and the Université Stendhal (Grenoble III). In discussions all parties agreed in principle to student exchanges. Attention was then turned towards the possibility of mutually-recognized double awards resulting from the programme of study. It was felt that this would help overcome the reluctance of employers to recognize the validity of other countries' qualifications and enhance the attractiveness of the Polytechnic's degree course to prospective students.

It was the intention to design a programme of study which would expose students to the language, culture and business practices of a major mainland European country and extend the amount and type of course material covered particularly in the areas of human resource management and business organization. It was also decided to include the possibility of a short placement in a company during the period of foreign study. The system of joint accreditation would work on the basis of mutual recognition of the rules, regulations and practices governing a course of study of all partner institutions. This was to be underpinned by detailed work to remove or overcome inconsistencies and operational problems. This is in practice an on-going programme which will require considerable discussion and joint working throughout the operation of the course. Clearly in these circumstances it was, and is, necessary to establish good working relations on a personal basis with, and between, key members of all institutions.

Following discussion and joint working, a mutually acceptable programme of study was constructed which fulfilled the national rules and regulations of all partners and allowed for the award of the qualification of the participating institution. All partner institutions then committed themselves to this double award programme and set about obtaining formal approval from validating bodies. The Polytechnic received approval in October 1989 with first intakes of students in September 1990. Partner institutions have all received approval in principle and are set for a first exchange of students in 1992.

The structure of the degree

In order to facilitate the double award and cover the necessary material it was crucial that this degree should be a four-year full time programme. This will include a full year of study and placement on the continent. The structure of the programme and the stages of the various awards is outlined in Appendix 1. The course of study which students follow is shown in Appendix 2.

Students must decide to follow either a French or a German route. Students who successfully complete the French route are awarded a CNAA degree, a Licence and a Maîtrise qualification. Students who successfully complete the German route are awarded a CNAA degree and a Diplom-Betriebswirt.

The future

It is anticipated that the running of this programme will occupy significant staff time and talent. The course development team is faced with a substantial staff development programme so as to develop their own foreign language competence and to increase the European base of all units in the degree programme. To assist in this the team is working on staff exchanges and joint research with partner institutions and other institutions on the mainland. The team has also begun discussions with Spanish institutions to expand the scheme. While this venture has not been brought to a successful conclusion to date it has opened the way for a long-term process of moving towards a truly European business qualification. This involves a lot of hard work and raises a lot of problems. However the rewards are great and the potential for the development of the staff involved is considerable.

Appendix 1

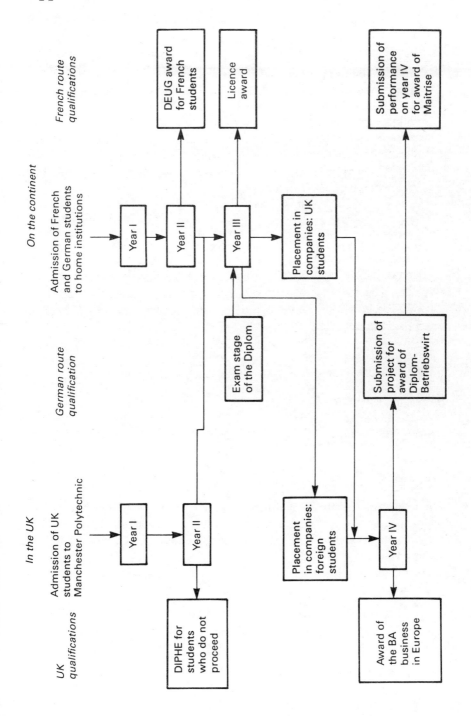

Appendix 2: BA (Hons) Business in Europe course structure and content

Year 1	Contact hours
German or French	6
Introduction to business law and comparative business law	2
Introduction to European economics	2
Introduction to European politics	2
Accounting and auditing in Europe	2
Applied information technology and statistics	2
Total	16

Year 2	Contact hours
German or French	6
Political and economic foundations of the European Community	2
Marketing in Europe	2
European law and accounting in Europe	2

and two options from:

International business	
Regional development in Western Europe	
Modern European economic development	4
Contemporary West European politics	
Business information systems	
Total	16

Year 3

In France or Germany studying language and culture of the country and business topics, eg decision-making in companies; finance; marketing; human resource management; exporting. All lectures, assessment and examinations will be in the language of the host country.

Approx 25

Year 4	*Contact hours*
German or French	4
Policy making in the European Community Project	2

and three options from:

Industrial economics
Industrial relations and The European
   labour market
Comparative public policy in Western Europe   8
Political economy of Southern Europe
Locational change in European industries and services
International money and financial markets
European marketing strategy
Management techniques
Either: European industrial
Marketing and selling
Or: Marketing research in Europe

                             Total   14

9 Developing a Coordinated Response in Further Education: the Cambridgeshire 1992 Project

Brian Bonney

The research projects

What has come to be known nationally as 'The Cambridgeshire 1992 Project' in fact comprises a sequence of three projects, funded by the Department of Employment Training Agency. The Project's embedding phase continues until August 1991. The outcomes of the initial research and development phase, undertaken in the four-month period January to April 1989 on a budget of just over £25,000, were first published in four volumes in 1989 (Cambridgeshire, 1989).

The research and development project aimed to initiate a model for national dissemination whereby the further education sector could:

- make itself aware of the implications and opportunities of the Single European Market (SEM) in work-related further education;
- assist industry and commerce to prepare for 1992 and beyond;
- prepare students for the post-1992 era.

These aims were clarified in the process of rewriting the bid. The original proposal was much more parochial in scope, being based on the scale of operation of the individual college from which the idea originated. The Training Agency saw the need for basic research and development on a national scale before committing funding to 1992 developments within colleges. Hence the proposal emerged as a project of national scope, funded through the Training Agency head office in Sheffield, and managed from there.

For some in Cambridgeshire this was seen at the time as a diversion from the project's original aims, but I believe that this involvement in national work has yielded a substantial pay-off in terms of the scale of developments now able to be implemented locally.

Research findings – industrial and commercial organizations

As part of the research methodology interviews were conducted in 24 industrial and commercial organizations from among the 57 that were invited to participate by letter and advance distribution of a question-naire. These ranged from small firms to multinationals and included firms of international accountants. The sample was selected for quality of information, and so the firms approached were identified from among those already having strong European connections and relevant training programmes of their own. They were not, therefore, necessarily the type of organization most likely to seek help from the further education sector. However the strategy employed was to establish instances of good practice from those already making progress in order better to assess the needs of those businesses requiring assistance from training providers.

Not surprisingly, the need for increased language skills, acquired within a cultural, vocational and/or professional context, emerged as the most immediate training requirement. However the need for knowledge and understanding of the changes associated with 1992 and their implications for business was often seen as more important. Many of the consequent skill requirements were not specifically SEM-related, but were identified as being needed in greater measure in the run-up to 1992 and beyond. Marketing, sales and distribution skills were the concern of many employers, with particular training needs identified in areas such as:

- assessing product suitability;
- marketing into Europe;
- knowledge of European markets;
- export/import administration;
- exploiting new markets.

Management and organizational skills were also a frequently perceived need, with a particular emphasis on:

- management development within a European strategic dimension;
- business organization skills;
- modifying work practices.

Commercial and financial practices were another perceived skill shortage area. Eighty per cent of the sample identified training needs in business methods and procedures, with many seeking enhanced knowledge of the accounting methods used in other EC countries.

Just prior to the survey, the DTI was claiming 90 per cent awareness of the meaning of 1992, as a result of its 'Europe Open for Business' campaign. However, the survey revealed a disturbing lack of perception among employers of the training needs arising in such areas as:

- tendering and public procurement;
- quality assurance and control;
- applications of new technologies (particularly information and communications technologies);
- personnel management;
- strategic planning;
- customer care.

These all clearly relate to the ability of a company to remain competitive in the wider European market. A continuing need for awareness-raising, particularly among smaller firms, was identified.

The SEM results from legislation. Knowledge of this legislation as it applies generally, and to specific sectors, was identified as another urgent training need. Particular concerns among employer respondents included knowledge of employment, competition, and consumer law. Access to a specialist in international law was a frequently stated requirement. A clear need emerged in employer perceptions, for knowledge of the more specific legal implications of the SEM, especially those relating to harmonization of standards in particular sectors, and registration (eg of agrochemicals and pharmaceuticals).

Research findings – colleges

A second component of the research methodology was a college survey which was conducted in two stages:

- an exploratory stage, in which issues were identified through discussions with senior staff in ten further and/or higher institutions;
- an interview and workshop stage, in which eight of the original ten colleges were revisited, to discuss issues in greater depth with groups of staff. Seven other institutions, not involved in the first phase, also participated but on a less formal basis.

It became clear that the SEM will create (and is creating) opportunities for further education colleges to meet new training needs. In particular:

- the immediate need for staff to be made aware of the general implications of the SEM to industry and commerce;

- the need to set up systems for monitoring progress towards completion of the SEM;
- the continuing need for colleges to make themselves more aware of the makeup of their local business communities, and the impact of the SEM measures upon them;
- the specific training needs to be met on a full-cost basis, such as:
  - awareness-raising in the local community,
  - language skills and cultural awareness training linked to particular applications (eg import/export administration and marketing skills),
  - intensive language courses, covering a wide range of languages not traditionally taught in schools,
  - knowledge of EC law as it applies to all, and to specific sectors.

Opportunities and challenges for colleges

Other opportunities exist for colleges to establish links and identify new student markets in other EC member states, and for setting up joint vocational programmes of study with partner institutions elsewhere in the EC. Colleges might also serve as access points for SEM-related information and advice in their local communities by establishing SEM-centres. This addresses the well-documented need for local businesses and individuals to have access to a 'one-stop shop', whereby any requirement for advice or information can be satisfied directly, or by signposting the client to an appropriate source.

There are organizational implications for the further education sector at all levels, whether institutional, local, regional or national in taking advantage of these opportunities. In reviewing these the Project made the following recommendations:

- colleges should make the SEM a priority in academic or business planning, prepare discussion and action documents, and set up college SEM coordinating teams or units with local collaboration as appropriate;
- local education authorities (LEAs) should encourage local collaboration through college consortia and/or a LEA coordinator, prepare a specific item on Europe (1992) within LEA strategic plans, and work with the emerging Training and Enterprise Councils (TECs) which will also have a strategic planning role;
- networking should be encouraged on regional, national and international scales, making use of EC funding opportunities where appropriate;
- colleges, LEAs and Regional Advisory Councils should link region-

ally with sectoral (industry-specific) collaboration, and develop regional or sectoral networks to act in a 'dating agency' or marketing capacity to assist in establishing links across Europe;

- study tours abroad should be encouraged for senior staff, using EC funding opportunities.

Although the Projects' fieldwork focused on the immediate updating and retraining needs in local industry, many knock-on effects for longer-term and broader-based curriculum development were identified. In particular the Project identified the need to:

- link closely SEM-related curriculum development to marketing, particularly given the countdown to 1992;
- encourage flexibility of opportunity for students/trainees, and to encourage the participation of older age groups, including women returners, in vocational education and training, given known demographic trends in Europe;
- encourage innovative, flexible learning opportunities, including self-access and open learning approaches;
- alert staff and students to the key role that information and communications technologies will play if the single market is to become a reality;
- establish computer networks between colleges and local firms, linked to similar networks elsewhere in Europe.

Further and higher education have their own specialized requirements for advice and information, and its needs have been less well served than those of industry. The Project therefore proposed the setting up of a national SEM centre for further and higher education, with local area or regional outlets as appropriate. The PICKUP Europe Unit has since emerged, with the support of the DES, and aims to fulfil this need as far as full-cost updating and retraining provision is concerned. How this concept might be developed to meet the full range of needs we originally envisaged is considered more fully below.

Dissemination and national networking

Following the completion of the fieldwork, further funding was approved by the Training Agency to disseminate the project findings nationally up to December 1989. In addition to the publication of the project documentation, this dissemination stage sought to:

- develop and update further the project findings;
- make contributions to conferences, workshops and seminars across the UK;

- work with LEAs and colleges on a consultancy basis;
- enable more specific staff development activity on specific aspects of the Project;
- work with Cambridgeshire schools-based staff so as to produce checklists appropriate to schools-sector developments.

The documentation was published in June 1989. It is now used for strategic planning purposes in colleges, LEAs, TECs and Regional Advisory Councils. Demand for the documents remains high, and continued sales have helped to offset costs once funding for dissemination ceased. National demand for conference and other contributions was greater than anticipated. Contributions were made to 32 events in the period April to December 1989 and demand continues. All this has raised the profile of the Project, providing further valuable contacts and sources of information, and another source of income to offset costs.

A key part of the Project's national dissemination has been, and continues to be, networking with other Training Agency-funded projects. I served on the steering group of the project 'A European Further Education Partnership' run by the Association of Principals of Colleges International. APC published a summary of our full report (APC, 1989). Bulletin no. 2 reports their own research findings, and surveys FE arrangements in Europe, arrangements for staff and student exchanges, and joint curriculum development exercises (Rust and Seabrooke, 1990). A further APC project, to broaden the investigation to include the industrial and commercial dimensions of curriculum development in Europe, has recently been approved.

The APC identified a need for a national centre for European vocational education and training. This would provide the focus for a network of regional and area centres to coordinate all European activities within the FE Sector – a broader remit than that of the PICKUP Europe Unit. A decision on establishing such a national unit depends upon clarification of the role of the PICKUP Europe Unit network, and the identification of the objectives of the emerging Training and Enterprise Councils in relation to the SEM.

However a regional Euro-unit concept has been piloted at the Sandwell College of Technology. The West Midlands Euro-Unit has operated since November 1989 and seeks to coordinate the activities of 59 colleges. It aims to provide an information base on the SEM, to promote the regional FE service across the EC, and to support curriculum exchanges with mainland Europe. The Unit works through a consortia of colleges, LEAs and TECs and so is concerned with the sharing of information and expertise on a regional scale. Whilst the West Midlands Euro-Unit has piloted the APC's concept of a regional centre, the Cambridgeshire

Project has piloted the concept of the more localized area centre, tied closely to the activities of TECs. APC sees the need for regional centres supported by area centres, the latter being sited in colleges or LEAs. The proposal for regional centres is to base them in independent units (as currently in the West Midlands), Regional Advisory Councils (to be piloted in Yorkshire and Humberside), or in a college (a proposal exists for such an arrangement in the South West of England). However, all these proposals must be judged in relation to the concurrent emergence of the DES-funded PICKUP Europe Unit.

The role of the PICKUP Europe Unit, as defined by the DES, is to:

- raise awareness within further and higher education of the training implications of the SEM;
- digest and provide information on the SEM for the specific use of the further and higher education audience;
- identify the scope for development in further and higher education provision related to SEM opportunities;
- disseminate good practice in the further and higher education sector.

The PICKUP Europe Unit is based at Southbank Polytechnic, the other main partners being the University of Bradford and Leeds Polytechnic, with the Spicers Eurocentre in Leeds as Senior Consultants. Further education interests are currently represented by Associate Membership (the Cambridgeshire colleges, Wakefield District College, and Croydon College). The Unit has invited bids from FHE institutions and consortia to set up regional centres, a number of which will be established within each of the regions covered by the PICKUP regional development agents. In turn, the successful regional centres will establish satellite centres (for instance in local FE colleges) to act as delivery points for the PICKUP Europe Unit service. The establishment of regional and satellite centres will be through franchising arrangements.

Clearly there is a parallel between the development of the PICKUP Europe Unit and the APC proposals currently being tested by Training Agency-funded pilot projects. The key differences are that the PICKUP Europe Unit aims to support both FE and HE in meeting the needs of industry and commerce, while the APC concept is solely FE-based, and seeks to address broader European curriculum issues, including the setting up of vocational education links across Europe. However, the scope for overlap of these two emergent networks is self-evident, and it would seem that rationalization will be necessary if wasteful duplication of effort, and confusion of purpose, is to be avoided.

The Cambridgeshire Project has exchanged information and ideas with other Training Agency-funded projects, including:

- 'Strategies for VET in Europe', directed from the European Institute of Educational and Social Policy in Paris. This aims to identify opportunities open to the UK FE system through examination, by a large team of practitioners, of the strategies for restructuring vocational education on an EC scale, and within member states. The team will identify changes in content, range and learning strategies for key occupational sectors, to be adopted in LEA development plans, and college curriculum programmes. This project is also supported by the FEU, which will undertake dissemination through bulletins, and the establishment of a network of UK practitioners.
- 'A College Strategy for the Provision of a European Curriculum for European Vocational Education', run at the De Havilland College in Hertfordshire. This aims to develop a curriculum model for dissemination, encompassing awareness-raising about 1992 for staff and students; a 1992 element in careers education programmes; incorporation of SEM core themes or units for all students; and strategies for the provision of Euro-courses and/or work experience in the Community.

Together these Training Agency-funded projects explore strategies for action at all levels from institutional, through LEA, regional, national and international, related to VET developments in the SEM context.

Concurrent with the Cambridgeshire Project, documents relating to SEM training needs were also being prepared by the FEU and by college groups set up by Yorkshire and Humberside Association of Further and Higher Education, the National Association of Teachers in Further and Higher Education and others. These contacts have proved invaluable in formulating the further development of the project in its third and current implementation phase.

Implementation within Cambridgeshire

This phase of the Project, entitled 'Providing the Competences Necessary to Prepare Employees for the Single European Market (1992)', started in January 1990 and is supported through the Training Agency Work Related Further Education Development Fund as a local embedding project until August 1991. Its aims are:

- in the short term, to help the five Cambridgeshire colleges to deliver successful full-cost adult training and updating, with particular reference to the competences required by employers and employees in preparation for the SEM;
- in the longer term, to incorporate European awareness and preparation into the mainstream work-related FE curriculum.

More specifically, the project objectives include:

- awareness-raising (particularly among small and medium-sized businesses in the locality) of the opportunities and implications of the SEM;
- development of a coordinated county strategy for responding to the training needs of local employers, relating to the SEM;
- development and marketing of appropriate course materials and facilities, with arrangements for evaluation and delivery;
- development of a county strategy for incorporation of a European element into the mainstream curriculum, taking account of the activities of examining, validation and accreditation bodies nationally and internationally.

In the role of Project Director, I am supported by a team of five college-based coordinators, each released for the equivalent of one day per week from their normal teaching duties. This team is applying strategies for action on two scales of operation – that of each individual college, and of the consortium as a whole. In the process, the merits of encouraging interaction between developments on these two scales of operation have been demonstrated.

The college-based coordinators are located in each of the five Cambridgeshire colleges:

Cambridgeshire College of Agriculture and Horticulture	(CCAH)
Peterborough Regional College	(PRC)
The Huntingdonshire College	(THC)
Isle College, Wisbech	(IC)
Cambridge Regional College	(CRC)

In what follows, they will be referred to by the respective college initials given above.

The activities of this team have to be seen in the context of a range of other projects operating within Cambridgeshire. A 1992 initiative cannot stand alone, and the team has been able to call upon the support of other groups in order to achieve action. Key examples of other LEA-managed development projects are:

- The Competence Base Curriculum Development and Recording Project. This project aims to provide, for each curriculum area in the county FE service, a vehicle for the coordination of curriculum planning and development, and a focus for staff development. It operates through eighteen curriculum development groups (CDGs), each of which undertakes curriculum audits detailing provision and resources in its own field. They monitor NVQ developments and prepare development plans for the introduction of NVQs for recommendation to colleges. They assess resources available for modular delivery, and plan for its introduction. They identify the concomitant staff development needs, and propose appropriate training opportunities for inclusion in the county staff development programme. Liaison with the CDGs therefore provides the 1992 team with effective channels through which to instil a 1992 element into curriculum planning and staff development county-wide.

- The Core Curriculum Project. This seeks to establish an agreed post-16 core curriculum for all full-time students, and to develop materials to aid its delivery, along with methods of recording and accrediting the core experience. An entitlement audit has been conducted country-wide. The need for a European element in the core area of economic, industrial and community awareness is receiving attention by liaison with the 1992 team.
- The Open Learning Project. This DES-funded project has stimulated the adoption of open learning (OL) as a mainstream mode of delivery. It has raised the competence of staff in such areas as finding and selecting OL packages and programmes; designing and developing OL materials; managing the resources of an OL operation; and providing appropriate administrative services. Staff development materials alerting staff to the implications of 1992 are in preparation through liaison with the 1992 team.
- A matrix operating on a county scale. Liaison work with other county groups reflects the county-wide dimension of our 1992 activities. Each of the college-based coordinators has a county-wide role in relation to selected curriculum areas in which he/she is conversant and a cross-curricular role in relation to developments in her/his own college.

County-wide responsibilities in particular curriculum areas are undertaken through liaison with the curriculum development groups. The project directors liaise directly with the coordinator of the CDG Project, attend meetings of the eighteen leaders of the CDGs and liaise directly with each other as appropriate. Periodic meetings are held between all county project directors to share ideas, report on progress, and identify opportunities for collaboration. This synergy between the diverse innovative activities within the county yields additional outcomes for each project which could not be achieved by each project working in isolation.

To encourage further a college dimension in the Project '1992 workshops' have been run in each college led by the respective college coordinator. This has enabled each college to formulate its own specific response to 1992 within the overall county strategy. Initially they have been largely of an awareness-raising nature, but college activities are now moving towards more specific action planning, involving college staff with interests spanning a range of curriculum areas, and cross-college responsibilities. The involvement of senior managers, affirming their commitment to European developments, has been of key importance.

Examples of developments so far instituted within colleges include:

- establishment at PRC (one of the larger colleges) of a 1992 Policy Committee involving senior management, and a 1992 Curriculum Committee with cross-college responsibilities;
- the setting up of information centres – as a separate unit at CRC, in the open learning area at PRC and as a section of the library at THC;
- the purchase of language tapes for the use of staff by open access at THC;
- organization of a 1992 seminar by business studies and travel and tourism students at CRC as part of an assignment;
- preparation of college 1992 strategies for consideration by college management (CRC and CCAH);
- development of a tutor package at IC for use as a 1992 awareness-raising resource for students;
- staff exchanges with a catering college in Holland, and contact made with a transnational European network (IC).

Such in-college developments are shared at monthly 1992 team meetings, so avoiding unnecessary duplication of effort. Colleges reserve the right to withhold specific details if a competitive advantage would be put at risk by disclosure of information. On the whole, however, free sharing of information and ideas has proved to have mutual advantage in these early developmental (and largely pre-competitive) stages. The dissemination of information by each coordinator within his/her college, and their establishment as contact persons for European matters, have quickly proved to be valuable assets, both within the college and for dealings with outside collaborators or clients.

Meeting industrial and commercial needs

Meeting the SEM-related training needs of local industrial and commercial communities is by far the most challenging aspect of the Project's response to 1992. The team is guided by earlier research and development findings and is involved at the college level in establishing closer working partnerships with business clients in order to:

- alert them to their own training needs, if they are to remain competitive;

- raise awareness of college staff to the implications of the SEM on local business.

The approach adopted has been to select samples of 12 or more small and medium-sized enterprises (SMEs) within the catchment of each college, and to undertake training needs analysis within these firms by semi-structured interviews, based on questionnaire materials. In this way the SEM acts as a lead activity in helping to raise the level of PICKUP work generally within the five colleges. Links with the PICKUP Europe Unit will help achieve PICKUP-related objectives, and help overcome the credibility problem that the FE service has faced in the past in this increasingly important area of work.

Staff development activity

Clearly a project of this sort is a staff development activity in itself, in particular for the coordinating team, but also for everyone else whom it seeks to influence. In the initial months, the staff development needs of the team itself were paramount, and each has undergone a programme of training in training needs analysis (TNA) techniques, and had the opportunity for sharpening presentational skills. This was to assist the team with local training needs surveys and to give confidence to undertake the task. The TNA training in particular led to the preparation of survey materials, project briefing sheets, and other necessary documentation/ publicity materials. Support from the local employer network proved valuable in targeting appropriate local firms.

In-college 1992 workshops were conducted at an early stage to raise the profile of the coordinators within their respective colleges, and of the project itself county-wide. These followed county awareness-raising events conducted mainly for senior LEA and college managers and county inspectors, during the Project's dissemination phase. Each college coordinator has undertaken an audit of staff expertise, experience and expectations in relation to the college/LEA response to 1992. These audits formed the basis for a programme of staff development activities for 1990/91 negotiated with the LEA, based in part upon the Local Education Authority Training Grants (LEATGs) Scheme National Priority Area funding but including local priorities identified through audit activity. The programme includes:

- A 1992 theme to be incorporated in a county Senior Staff Conference.
- Specific funding allocated to work with the curriculum development groups to initiate developments across the curriculum, including language and European awareness modules, knowledge of the effects of EC legislation, 1992 in the core curriculum, and the sharing of

experience in setting up links across the EC. In particular, a 'roadshow' which will visit each college led by the 1992 team with contributions from those CDGs making good progress in this area. This 'road show' will pass on experience from the leading CDG to all areas of college work, and establish more specific objectives for the in-college SEM teams, and the CDGs themselves.

- Cascading the experience of the 1992 and PICKUP teams within each college, based on the training needs surveys undertaken in local industry, so as to involve more staff actively.
- In-college seminars on developing short course and flexible learning provision, to initiate the development of training packages appropriate to local industry, and staff development.
- In-college workshops on resource issues and preparation of bids for external funding to be led by LEA and college staff with relevant experience.
- encouragement of language learning by staff, through open access to language learning resources, and infill on courses available in the colleges. Enthusiasm among staff for learning languages was a prominent feature of in-college audits, and this is being encouraged.

Broader perspectives and future plans

A County 1992 Action Group was set up in June 1989, and meets twice each term. The Group acts as a focus for collection and dissemination of information and guidance between the LEA and its institutions in the primary, secondary, further, and community education sectors, regarding the implications of the SEM and the broader European perspective. The Project has been involved with the group from the outset leading to the production of an awareness raising document on 1992 for staff in schools. The document was launched in February 1990 at a county 1992 event for secondary school heads, county inspectors and officers. The event included an exhibition of documentary, audio-visual and software materials. The outcomes of workshops held at the event are being used to formulate a county strategy for linking schools and FE developments.

The Action Group has spawned a TVEI County 1992 Group, which is looking at linking their activities with comparable activities elsewhere in Europe. More recently, a reconstituted schools working group has been formed to plan a support programme to stimulate activity throughout the educational service.

It is not the prerogative of the Cambridgeshire Project to organize and participate in European links: often these are best left to individual initiatives. However the Project has attempted to keep in touch with such developments within the county and facilitate the process of setting up new links. As a performance criteria the team is seeking to set up, and find funding to support, at least one new link for each college in the first year of the implementation phase. The national profile attained in the research and development phase of the Project is of great value in this respect.

In February 1990, members of the County 1992 Action Group visited Brussels to meet with various EC funding and networking agencies. This proved a valuable staff development opportunity, and provided an up-to-date appreciation of the purposes and present priorities of such agencies.

Cambridgeshire has established links through town and city twinning arrangements, and personal contacts abroad. There is also experience at the county level of exchange and study visits. For instance:

- The Cambridgeshire-Kreis Viersen Exchange Programme, first established in 1971, has involved over 10,000 adults and young people from the county in visits and exchanges as members of school and college groups, youth clubs, adult education classes, sports and cultural activity groups. The Cambridgeshire Project is seeking to extend these links to include joint vocational programmes of study, incorporating work experience on an exchange basis as an integral part of the programmes.
- Study visits are in progress, and should lead to more substantial student and staff exchanges, with VET institutions offering vocational education in Antwerp and Lyons, supported through the Mainframe/PETRA programme on behalf of the FEU.

Funding to support such activity into Eire, Spain, France, and elsewhere is being actively sought. Such activity helps the 'internal marketing' of the Project, provides great motivation for staff in all curriculum areas to get involved, and yields what people expect of a 'European project' – direct experience of, and contact with, educational systems elsewhere in Europe.

We have also contributed an FE dimension to recent activities of the UK section of the European Association of Teachers, and we represent the UK section on the EC-funded international project, 'Vocational Education and Mobility', run from Brussels. Thus, the Project has achieved some international penetration, and it is proposed that it should assist the UK section of EAT in organizing an international conference on vocational education – likely to be held in Strasbourg in 1991.

The LEA has an active commitment through its colleges to work within a European framework, to increase the level of full-cost adult training activity, and to continue this activity after Training Agency pump-priming is completed. It is therefore active in providing staff development programmes to ensure staff have the ability to prepare business plans, set market prices, and to retain and reinvest income. A business plan for the

Project will be produced to take account of income earning activities generated on two levels:

- Work undertaken entirely within a college, though stimulated by the Project's activities, to be treated as part of the college's income-earning activity.
- Income earned centrally by the Project, through such activities as consultancy, contributions to out-county events, and publications, to be accounted for through a centrally held Project budget.

The provision of training needs analysis services to local industry is seen as a marketable and remunerative activity and the operation of a county unit dedicated to TNA work is a feasible longer-term outcome of the Project.

Associate membership of the PICKUP Europe Unit supports the colleges' own PICKUP activities, while enabling the Project to serve in an advisory capacity representing FE interests, and supporting dissemination activities. Already the Unit has supported two new programmes:

- more detailed TNA work within the electronics-based industries in and around Cambridgeshire, to provide data for dissemination through the national network;
- updating and remarketing of the Project's research and development documentation under the PICKUP Europe Unit banner.

Lesson learnt

The Project has been an interesting odyssey; its course is far from complete, and its future directions are not easy to predict. After eighteen months activity the Project finds itself involved in areas of work, local to international in scale, which could not have been predicted at the outset.

Some key lessons learned are:

- the value of work at a national level in achieving more parochial objectives locally, and in generating new funding opportunities, from UK national or EC sources;
- the scale of the task of coordinating European developments, and the need to develop systems for channelling information, and recruiting expertise across the curriculum;
- the merit of a county matrix model in coping with the scale of the task;
- the need to involve everyone within a college, and convince them that European matters are not just the concern of the language or European studies specialists;
- the value of a team within each college to provide a point of contact for all concerned with Europe;

- the need to provide scope for individual and college initiative (on a competitive basis if appropriate) while supporting developments through an overall county strategy and central coordination;
- the suitability of the Cambridgeshire system for instilling a European dimension into the planning processes of the emergent TECs;
- the usefulness of the PICKUP approach as a lead activity informing longer-term and broader curriculum development, affecting all sectors of education and training.

In our early research and development work a quick lesson learned was to stop thinking of 1992 in terms of 'threats', and to speak in terms of 'opportunities and implications'. I am optimistic that the county model presented here, viewed in the context of the larger-scale national and international networks which can be harnessed to support it, provides an effective response to the challenge of Europe.

References

Association of Principals of Colleges International (1989) *Vocational Education and Training for the Single European Market*, APC Bulletin no. 1, June, London

Bonney Rust, W and Seabrooke, G (1990) *A European Fuller Education Partnership*, Association of Principals of Colleges International, Bulletin no. 2, London

Cambridgeshire County Council (1989) *The Single European Market: Opportunities and Implications for the Further Education Sector*, Four volumes, Cambridgshire C.C. Education Services

10 Responding to the Free Movement of Professional Labour: Curriculum Developments in Diagnostic Radiography

Geoff Bemrose and Christine Dobson

Radiographic education – development of a graduate profession

Radiography, which encompasses both the diagnostic and therapeutic branches, is a relatively new profession with its roots established during the turn of the twentieth century. Since that time there has been dynamic change both in the education and clinical practice aspects of radiography and these changes will continue into the future. This is due in part to the rapid advances in technology and in medical science which have taken place. Diagnostic radiography provides physicians and surgeons with pictorial evidence of disease or injury which aids diagnosis. Modern technology means this is no longer confined to the production of an x-ray film, but includes the use of ultrasound, computed tomography scanning, digital imaging, radionuclide and magnetic resonance imaging.

During the first half of the twentieth century radiography training consisted of largely practical training with most instruction taking place in the x-ray room. This was supplemented by lectures on the theoretical basis of radiography. However, by the 1950s changes in technology and practice resulted in the profession becoming larger and more diversified. This increased the level of knowledge and skills required and so had a direct effect on radiography education. The theoretical aspects formed a larger and more important part of the course than previously and schools of radiography were established in the UK to offer this component to students. The clinical placement element was retained, but its nature has changed gradually to one of providing the necessary learning experience and clinical practice for the student, rather than the original concept that students were part of the work-force.

Schools of radiography offered day-release of one to three days a week with the remainder of the time spent in the x-ray department. The schools during this period were small monotechnic institutions which developed in a rather piecemeal fashion across the country, usually attached to large hospitals and originally set up to meet the training needs of a particular area. There were no links with mainstream education during this period, neither with individual institutions nor on a national level with the Department of Education and Science. It was, and still is in England, the Department of Health which provides student bursaries and so maintains its influence on human resource planning.

Until recently all radiographers have qualified to practise through successful completion of the Diploma of the College of Radiographers which automatically confers state registration from the Council of Professions Supplementary of Medicine. The syllabus for the diploma is laid down by the College of Radiographers and relies upon national terminal examinations for its assessment. The course requires two 'A' levels as a condition of entry and is three years in length. Students receive a Department of Health bursary, calculated in the same way as a local education authority grant, and have full student status. In the last decade there has been a movement to place radiography schools on a sounder educational footing. This includes rationalization of schools, the adoption of a block system format and links with education. The latest development in radiography education in the United Kingdom is the advent of degree courses leading to a Bachelor of Science Honours degree in Radiography. It is possible, and many would say desirable, that as a result of these first degree courses radiography may well become a graduate profession by the year 2000. This development has meant closer links with mainstream higher education and brings considerable benefits to radiography as a profession.

The need for degree courses has been a result of the rapid advances in medical science and the increasing sophistication of technology available to the Health Service which is changing the demands placed upon the professionals who deliver the radiography service. The professions supplementary to medicine, which include radiography, now more than ever need to develop new skills and adapt their expertise to novel environments. There is a need for them to develop their abilities as decision-makers and innovators in order that they can fully contribute to the health care team and provide the accurate information required by clinicians. The diagnostic radiographer is particularly affected by these developments. The technical advances in areas such as computer-aided imaging techniques, new modalities and interventional radiography require an increase in both practical and intellectual skills. Radiographers must be continually aware of the safety implications of their work and this requires an ability to interpret new safety legislation and to apply new codes of practice in order to ensure maximum protection for their patients.

These technical and legislative developments are matched by an awareness in patients which increases their expectations of care and treatment and demands a high level of counselling and interpersonal skills from the radiographer. A graduate qualification will provide the best possible preparation for the radiographer to meet these developments. It will develop flexible and adaptable individuals with intellectual, managerial and practical skills of the highest standard. The graduate radiographer will be able to address problems, improve practice, and carry out research in order to benefit the patient both in diagnosis and care.

The European context

Radiographic education in the United Kingdom has tended to be among the most developed within the European Community, and the graduate status now being attained places it in a unique position. There is tremendous variation throughout the countries of the European Community in the way that radiographers are trained and qualify, which ranges from no official training in Belgium to the three-year courses which exist in Denmark, Ireland, Netherlands and the United Kingdom. It is in this context that the Suffolk College and the Ipswich School of Radiography have both sought and gained accreditation through the Council for National Academic Awards (CNAA) for a BSc (Hons) Degree in Radiography.

Current developments in radiography education coincide with an era of radical change for all vocational education in the UK, most notably the necessity of rewarding prior experience and learning; and the need to make education and training more accessible, particularly to the mature returner and individuals with a non-traditional educational background. Additionally, and significantly, the removal of employment barriers in 1992 will allow transnational exchange of professionals throughout the European Community so encouraging a European standard for vocational education and professional accreditation.

This period of radical change provides the perfect base for incorporating new strategies and concepts into a transnational approach to radiographic education. This perception forms the basis of the work undertaken by the Suffolk College and the Ipswich School of Radiography to establish the current status of radiographic education and training across the EC and integrate this into the curriculum of the newly validated degree course. To facilitate this, initial research has begun to review course structures and content reflecting time of study, the balance between clinical education and academic study, and mode of assessment; and to define the outcomes of education and training in terms of preparedness and competence to undertake diagnostic radiography. The current nature of radiographic qualifications is being established and their status in a national and international framework determined. Common themes and core studies are being identified which could be utilized to form the basis of a transnational exchange programme, and where possible examples of good and interesting practice are being highlighted.

Areas for curriculum development

Initial research has demonstrated a number of general trends in vocational education which will need to be incorporated in the continuing process of curriculum development for radiographic education. The first is an increased requirement for accessibility to courses, particularly for mature candidates and returners, which is frequently facilitated by the development of modular programmes and the award of credits for the successful completion of whole or part modules. Second, the value associated with the enhanced flexibility provided for the student by credit accumulation and transfer, and similar systems, leading to the award of a diploma or degree. Credit accumulation and transfer (CATS) may be seen as a process whereby qualifications, part-qualifications and learning experiences are given appropriate recognition and credit to enable students to progress in their studies without necessarily having to repeat material or levels of study; transfer within and between courses; and gain further educational experience and qualifications without undue loss of time. Properly employed a CATs scheme can offer an effective, learner-centred approach to maximizing accumulated educational capital. Clearly a CATs scheme can enable the transfer of credit across national and international boundaries, and an approach of this kind is currently being piloted through the EC's ERASMUS-linked European Community Course Credit Transfer System.

Third is the need to recognize alternative qualifications for initial entry to radiography education. In particular this will refer to the role of:

- the accreditation of prior learning – particularly quantitative methods of assessing skills and expertise developed in the clinical environment;

- access course provision and its relevance to current trends in education and employment;
- a mechanism for granting exemption from parts of a professional qualificatory course.

Fourth is the importance of strategies for the introduction and development of alternative curriculum delivery methods. This is likely to include the identification of innovative teaching and learning strategies and the role of non-traditional delivery methods such as open and distance learning, computer-aided techniques and expert systems.

In all cases it is essential that developments in curriculum accessibility, flexibility and innovation reflect the needs of the profession, the professional groups and legislative bodies such as the College of Radiographers and the Radiographers Board of the Council of Professions Supplementary to Medicine.

Implications of the free movement of professionals

Central to this work will be the impact of the European Community and particularly the creation of a Single European Market with its concomitant removal of barriers to the free movement of professional labour. The fact that, by law, a qualified radiographer from a member state will be eligible to practise their profession in any other member state is indicative of the critical need to include a comprehensive and coherent European perspective into the future curriculum of radiographic education and training programmes.

To support this development our research activity which is being funded by the College of Radiographers will address three main areas:

- the current status of education and training for diagnostic radiographers and the role of the qualified radiographer, both in the United Kingdom and in European member states;
- the commonality between educational programmes for radiographers across the European Community and the potential for this commonality to be used as the basis of a transnational credit transfer system;
- the identification of the issues which will need to be addressed by professional bodies in accepting radiographers trained in other member states as practitioners and mechanisms which can facilitate decision-making on individual cases.

Each of these areas will ultimately influence the nature of the curriculum and its delivery in radiographic education. The specific implications for the curriculum are being established and are likely to involve:

- a review of professional qualificatory course structure and content reflecting time of study, the balance between clinical education and academic study, and the modes of assessment;

- a definition of the outcomes of education and training in terms of preparedness and competence of the individual to undertake the duties of a diagnostic radiographer;
- a review of entry qualifications and accessibility to professional educational programmes. Particular emphasis will be placed on mechanisms for the accreditation of prior learning, particularly in aspects of clinical practice.

In order to obtain accurate information from other European member states a network of contacts is being established. This network is not only providing a base for the collection of data, but also assisting in the comparative studies which will be necessary to address the comparability of the role of radiographers, the aims of educational programmes and the preparedness and competence of individuals to practise in other member states. It is clear that within a single state a number of parties will influence the education of the radiographer, in particular: the professional bodies/government agencies; the deliverers of radiographic education; the radiographer him/herself.

This initial phase will allow the identification of common practice between member states, particularly in terms of the aims of educational programmes and the common themes and core studies which may be apparent in courses. Such commonality will be investigated to assess whether it could form the basis of transnational exchange programmes allowing students to participate in training in more than one member state and receive credit for all academic and clinical work undertaken irrespective of its location. More importantly for transnational professional labour mobility our work will establish the level to which educational studies in one member state may be credited in other states. This will allow an initial determination of 'competence to practise' and the requirements for further study which could arise from the transnational mobility of professional radiographers.

The outcomes of this research will allow the identification of common academic and clinical components within radiographic education across the European member states. The logical next step will then be to address the manner in which this information can be used to provide a transnational credit system which will allow the accreditation of education and training in different member states. Ultimately this could lead to a European framework for radiographic education which should reflect the advanced state of educational practice in the UK. This phase would also need to identify areas of shortfall in the educational programmes of member states. It is essential that a mechanism for accommodating such shortfalls be available in the form of a range of short courses and intensive training programmes which would meet the varied needs of professional bodies and individuals across the EC.

Initiatives such as the one described can attract support from the European Community notably through the ERASMUS programme where the resources will be used to encourage universities and other higher educational providers of different member states to establish inter-university cooperation programmes (ICPs). The European aspect of the research has already engendered staff mobility between member states and the identification of course components which will encourage student mobility. The network of European partners will ultimately lead to an ICP supporting the joint development of new curricular using data derived from the current research. This joint curriculum development will not only encourage academic recognition between member states and hence facilitate professional mobility, but also stimulate new curriculum delivery methods as well as strategies aimed at building a European dimension into the core content of professional qualificatory courses.

The imminence of 1992 and the associated potential for transnational exchange of the European workforce pose significant questions for all professions, but particularly those associated with patient care in the clinical environment. Government agencies and professional bodies will need to determine the competence of individuals trained in other member states to practise within their country. Where these decisions indicate a requirement for further training or experience it will be necessary to have a framework which will allow this to be delivered effectively in a short timescale. Our work has been designed to provide a basis upon which recommendations may be made to address these critical issues.

11 Promoting Initiatives in European Partnership: the Workers' Educational Association

Mel Doyle

The 'right' to vocational education and training

In May 1989 the European Commission issued its proposals for a European Community Charter of Fundamental Social Rights as part of the continuing dialogue over 1992 and the creation of the Single European Market. Importantly for UK organizations and institutions involved in educational provision for the trade union movement, the proposals referred to vocational training in ways which were consistent with the known views of the European Trade Union Confederation (ETUC). The ETUC is strongly committed to the recognition of vocational training as a social right in the 'New Europe'.

The Commission proposed that all workers in the EC should have the right to continue their vocational education and training throughout their working lives. The Commission has argued that public authorities, employers and trade unions should set up continuous and permanent training schemes, whereby all employees in the Community can receive retraining (through leave for training purposes) for the improvement of existing skills or for the acquisition of new skills, especially in response to the demands of technological change.

The new technology needs of industry have had a major influence on policy makers in Brussels in the development of their training policy options. This emphasis is wholly consistent with the products of the continuing dialogue between European employers and trade unions.

In a June 1989 communication from the Commission to the Council of Ministers, entitled 'Education and Training in the European Community: Guidelines for the Medium Term, 1989–92', the education and training implications of technological change were indicated clearly:

Over the next four-year period, the Commission considers that to make progress in mastering technological change, it will be essential to develop a coherent view of the introduction of the new technologies at all stages of the education and training process. To this end, a three-pronged approach has already been established by the Community institutions:

1. the need to improve university-industry collaboration so as to ensure that advanced training programmes are designed to take account of new skills needs and the interdisciplinary challenges of technological change;
2. the need to provide both the existing workforce and new workers with opportunities for training and retraining and to acquire new types of qualifications as the boundaries between jobs become more and more blurred under the pressures of technological change;
3. the need to exploit new technologies during the period of full-time compulsory education and initial training both in terms of curriculum content and new approaches and methodologies for learning, particularly within the framework of improved school-industry relations. (CCM, 1989)

There are a number of strategic themes which run through the Commission's training policies. Firstly, there has been encouragement for the integration of young people into the working environment by ensuring that they have the right to receive training after the completion of compulsory education. Secondly, cooperation at university level has been generated through the continued development and refinement of the ERASMUS and COMETT programmes. The objective is that by 1992, 10 per cent of all students will be following courses which, at least, are partially in an institution in another member state, or in a company in another member state.

Thirdly, the problem of mobility of qualified people has encouraged the Council of Ministers to adopt a directive on 'a general system for recognition of higher education diplomas awarded on completion of professional education and training of at least three years duration' (*OJEC*, 1989).

Fourthly, the proposed Social Charter, confirming the right of workers in non-professional occupations to improve their skills, acquire new skills, and gain leave to do so, has encouraged the European Centre for the Development of Vocational Training (CEDEFOP) to consider the production of a European vocational training card, validating the qualifications of the holder for recognition and use throughout the Community.

Finally, it has been appreciated that without the parallel development of language skills within the work-force many of the strategic initiatives which together will sustain the single market will be limited in their impact. The LINGUA programme has special significance in this context.

The response of the Workers' Educational Association

Thus vocational training is placed high on the European agenda for the 1990s. Importantly, the Workers' Educational Association's (WEA) response to the variegated issues takes note, in large part, of how British trade unions see their role in the training debate.

In a recent study of 1992, a WEA pamphlet saw the issues for British trade unions in the following terms:

> In the UK there is almost a decade of past training initiatives which have successfully kept the UK at, or close to, the bottom of the training league. The lack of training and its poor quality, requires trade unions comprehensively to examine the type of training they would want for their members. Is job specific training needed? Is more career development structured training, or industry-specific, or company-specific training needed? If it is a combination, then what type of combination?
>
> Trade unions can take a pro-active role to find out what their members require and then demand that the Community's programmes on training, and associated funding, take the requirements of workers fully into account. The Social Charter specifically refers to 'leave for training purposes', which raises the question of the definition of training purposes . . . The Charter seems to place special emphasis on training for skills in the light of technical development, but this is not necessarily incompatible with training related to understanding workplace change. . .
>
> Some trade unions have been successful in negotiating with employers for money specifically allocated for workers' training. This should be pursued by all unions, but particularly those organizing in multinational companies. It is compatible with the extension of collective bargaining into new areas which the social dialogue favours. (Ash, 1989)

Importantly, in assessing the contribution which it can make to equipping British trade unionists to play a fully active role in the Europe of the 1990s, the WEA has chosen to address those factors which historically have precluded effective participation. In summary form these are questions of British cultural insularity and the absence of linguistic skills which are associated with this phenomenon.

Developing European partnerships

The WEA has started from the advantageous position of having constitutional and organizational links with the majority of Britain's trade unions, which underpin a substantial presence in both the Trade Union Congress (TUC) regional educational scheme and the educational provision of many individual trade unions at national and local level. Furthermore, the WEA is connected internationally with the main providers of workers' education in the member states of the EC through its membership of the International Federation of Workers' Educational Associations (IFWEA) and through other bilateral and multilateral arrangements.

These 'Europartners' have provided access to training debates which otherwise would have been denied to the WEA. As well, they have offered practical support for the development and consideration of the international programmes of workers' education which the WEA is engaged in. Perhaps the most important contact has been with organizations in France, Belgium and the Federal Republic of Germany, although the potential of building new relationships elsewhere should not be ignored. Within this context avenues of cooperation are now opening with Spain and Denmark.

Generally speaking the European partners fall into two categories: national voluntary organizations active in workers' education ('sister' organisations to the WEA), such as Arbeit and Leben in the Federal Republic, Culture et Liberté and Leo Lagrange in France, and Centrale voor Socialistisch Cultuurbeleid in Belgium; and national trade union centres in Spain, France and the Federal Republic.

Currently the WEA is engaged in discussions with French, Belgium and German organizations and with the European Commission on the possibility of a curriculum development and in-service training project in workers' education focusing on 1992. It aims to examine the economic, social and cultural effects of the Single European Act, and the process of harmonization which the Act is designed to extend. A central concern is the addressing of issues of inter-dependence between nations. Its objectives of developing a curriculum base, in-service training approaches, and furthering European cooperation among teachers in workers' education has led to an early initiative in the field of information exchange.

In June 1990 a four-day international seminar was hosted by the WEA in Manchester on the theme of 'International Technology and European Cooperation in Workers' Education'. Representatives from workers' education organizations in nine European countries were present (Belgium, Denmark, France, Federal Republic of Germany, Ireland, Norway, Spain, Sweden and the United Kingdom). Financial support was received from Manchester City Council and simultaneous interpretation provided in English, French, German and Spanish. The main agenda was the establishment of a permanent network for efficient and cost-effective communications between workers' education organizations throughout Europe, allowing improved access to information and the development of integrated programmes of educational activities. That seminar provided hands-on experience of the GeoNet/Poptel database, notice board and electronic mail systems which currently link many trade union centres and community and campaigning organizations throughout the world. These are early days for assessing the viability of building permanent communication in this way, but the advance of information technology is such that a clear opportunity is offered by this form of networking.

The first visible forms of international cooperation in educational provision between the WEA and its European partners have been in the field of language training. The Communication from the Commission to the Council referred to earlier highlighted the problems associated with the low level of foreign language skills among Europe's workers:

> 1992 has helped to put the spotlight on the learning of foreign languages as the essential part of European education and training. Indeed the lack of people capable of working through the medium of Community languages other than their own is a crucial constraint to the completion of the Internal Market. It is also a handicap to the increasing business and trading connections within the Community. (CCM, 1989)

The importance of language training

Undoubtedly 1992 has begun to shape the WEA's attitudes to education and training priorities. The WEA's National Biennial Conference, held in April 1989, called upon the Association to respond urgently to the educational needs of working people arising from the process of European integration. By September 1989, the WEA had begun its first international partnership arrangements for the provision of 20 bank employees from the Federal Republic of Germany. The success of this venture has led to the WEA's German partners, Arbeit and Leben, asking the WEA to provide further English language training schools. Similar arrangements are under negotiation with French partners. Significantly, organizations from nations outside the Community as well are beginning to avail themselves of WEA provision. Arbetarnas Bildnings Forbund in Sweden and the Karl Renner Institute in Austria have agreed programmes of English language training with the WEA for Swedish and Austrian trade unionists respectively.

With this programme of 'in-coming' language training schools now well underway, the WEA has taken the first steps in providing foreign language training programmes for British trade unionists in Europe. The WEA's intention in 1990 and 1991 is to develop its organizational capacity, curriculum base, teaching skills and evaluation processes in foreign language training for British trade unionists. This began with a training programme of two schools in late 1990, one held in France and one in the Federal Republic of Germany, each of seven days' duration. The WEA's partners in these programme arrangements are Association Roudel and Arbeit and Leben. If successful, a larger programme is anticipated for 1991.

Importantly participants are being recruited without foreign language skills, which has important implications for the form which each training programme can take. The WEA's objectives for these student groups are as follows:

- to break down barriers of cultural insularity;
- to increase awareness of the single market;
- to appreciate the value of European partnership and cooperation;
- to appreciate the importance of foreign language skills;
- to develop basic foreign language skills;
- to provide participants with the confidence to develop further their foreign language skills.

These objectives imply that the programmes must be located within social and cultural contexts that are readily accepted by participants. Consequently it is recognized that this form of language training must have immediate relevance to the needs of participants as trade unionists, while the language tutors engaged must appreciate the trade union context of the provision as well as being technically competent as language trainers.

Currently both 'in-coming' and 'out-going' programmes have been developed on a self-financing basis. This places an enormous resource restraint on the WEA and its partners and is likely to be the major limitation on future growth and development. Importantly therefore, access to external funding is an urgent requirement. Potentially the most likely source of financial support is the EC's LINGUA programme. Certainly the WEA's activities are consistent with the broad aims of LINGUA which are 'to encourage a quantitative and qualitative improvement in knowledge of foreign languages with a view to developing skills as regards communication within the Community'.

Of the five main areas of 'Action' under this programme the WEA is currently seeking support under Action One (measures to promote in-service training) and Action Three (measures to provide knowledge of modern languages used in work relationships and in economic life). If such support is forthcoming, then the WEA can confidently enter the 1990s contributing much to the development of workers' education within Europe.

References

Ash, N (1989) *'1992': The Single European Market*, Workers Educational Association, Studies for Trade Unionists, vol. 15, no. 58, London

Communication from the Commission to the Council of Ministers (1989) *Education and Training in the EC: Guidelines for the Medium Term, 1989–92*, June 1989, Brussels

Official Journal of the European Communities (1989), 'Council Directive of 21 December 1988 on a general system for the recognition of higher education diplomas awarded on completion of professional education and training of at least three years' duration', no. L19/16, 24 January, HMSO, London

12 Learning from Experience: a European Partnership in the Agricultural Sector

Stefan Drew

This short case study has been designed to raise points and issues which need to be addressed by institutions offering vocational education as they prepare and plan for the impact of the Single European Market. The perspective offered is one drawn from experience in industry and shaped by the exciting and dynamic changes created by the Education Reform Act, by the run up to 1992, and by an awareness of the rapidly developing situation in Eastern Europe.

The partnership project

The partnership described here is based on the concept that a network of colleges across Europe can work together, to their mutual benefit, to provide not only traditional staff and student exchanges but can also act as an agent for change. The partnership project has provided a European referral service for research, consultancy and professional updating across a series of vocational sectors encompassed within l'industrie agro-alimentaire – the agriculture and food industry – from seed to plate. Any arrangement of this kind must have a facilitation unit in each member state linked not only to each other but also to a network of providers in their home territory. This approach recognizes that, in the agricultural sector at least, no single institution is likely to be in a position to respond successfully to the range of likely international client demand generated by the Single European Market. It also acknowledges that much vocational education, particularly PICKUP-type, will be potentially suitable for clients in all EC member states wherever it is originally designed.

The origins of the project lie with a visit to England and Wales in 1987 by a group of senior educationalists and trainers in agriculture from the

Rhône-Alp region of France, an area particularly rich in agriculture and horticulture product units, food processing and manufacturing, food cooperatives and allied industries many of which are international. The visiting group had targeted Cambridge as an area with which it wished to work and had arranged to meet key people from a range of public and private sector organizations. At the Cambridge College of Agriculture and Horticulture (CCAH) introductions were made, tours of the college and local area undertaken, and proposals exchanged. One such proposal was for some form of networking between colleges, research facilities and industry. This was worked up as a project which now spans six member states (Eire, France, Greece, Italy, Spain and the UK) and will ultimately cover all twelve members of the EC.

During the initial meeting a rapport was established between the then principal of CCAH and the director of the Institute Supérieur D'Agriculture Rhône-Alp, part of the Catholic Institute in Lyon, despite the fact that they shared only a few words of each other's languages. A further meeting was planned for a few months hence in Lyon. The meeting in Lyon was attended by a senior management team from CCAH in addition to the chairman of governors. The French hosts arranged for opinion-formers to be present, the media to cover the event and for visits and meetings to take place. Progress was thus assured on the basis of a senior managerial commitment to effective joint working. To seal further the developing arrangement the principal invited the director to return to the UK and to stay in his home for a holiday. For his part the director proposed a staff and student exchange arrangement between the two institutions.

I was seconded to teach English in the Agriculture Faculty in Lyon the following autumn while the French Professeur d'Anglais reciprocated at CCAH. While seconded I was able to continue planning the project and at that time it was decided to apply for funding from the European Community under the COMETT scheme. A student exchange was planned by each partner with a number of study tours arranged for private sector vocational education and training providers from the Rhône-Alp area to visit Cambridge for professional updating in subjects as diverse as the provision of bed and breakfast by farmers at the French end of the Channel tunnel, to 1992 orientation courses for members of French cooperatives and local chambers of agriculture.

During early 1989 I visited Lyon again as leader of a study tour which included Paris and Geneva in its itinerary. On this occasion the British students stayed with fellow students from the Catholic Institute while in Lyon so as to keep costs down. As part of the reciprocal visit French students stayed in CCAH's hall of residence.

At this stage both the principal of CCAH and I made career moves which potentially left the project without a steer. However following discussions with the new principal of CCAH it was agreed that I would take the management of the project with me to my new college keeping both UK institutions involved in the initiative. Consequently I arranged for the French group to visit the UK again to meet with the growing number of people that by this time were becoming involved in the project and to present the bid for EC support being made through the COMETT programme. There followed an international launch of the network in Lyon during February 1990 at which representatives from each of the member institutions met for the first time allowing the development of a common perspective and the further development of shared ownership of the project.

At this meeting a European Training Association was formed under French law with all participant organizations joining. A press conference announcing this initiative was held. With this launch the real vocational education and training work began. French sandwich-year students were placed in UK companies, English language training was organized for employees from France in the UK, international conferences were arranged, and a substantial body of other work undertaken. In August 1990 support through the COMETT programme was received reinforcing the commitment to enhance and extend this increasingly valuable partnership arrangement.

Issues arising from the project

A range of points and issues arise from the experience outlined briefly in this case study and these are discussed below.

A sense of European vision, clear institutional priority (probably explicit in a corporate statement of purpose), and personal contact and rapport are the keys to effective transnational work, particularly among senior managers. Realistically it is difficult to build lasting and successful links if these are not achieved. For this project it was felt to be important to have the support of all the college senior management team and governors, hence the reason for their involvement at an early stage, giving ownership to them and smoothing the path for future collaboration. It also emphasized that overseas travel is not a holiday but can be gruelling! Nonetheless it must be recognized that proposals presented by, or given to, potential partner institutions within the EC are often misunderstood due to cultural or procedural differences. One might imagine that putting two senior college managers together would facilitate an understanding, if not acceptance, of each other's perspectives. Experience with this project suggests that this is often not so. It is necessary to question every assumption at all stages. The problem goes beyond that of language, which in itself is a minor problem, to one of cultural understanding. It's worth stressing that this project has generated success without significant access to foreign language skills.

In terms of breadth of curriculum and research and consultancy services I strongly believe that no single institution can deal successfully with a field as vast as the agricultural industry. This has been a primary reason for the networking project. It is clear that many PICKUP-type products will be suitable wherever designed in the EC for use in all member states, particularly when they are at a more basic or fundamental level. However differences in national culture and educational expectation should be actively considered when designing or selling educational or training provision. Presentation styles, modes of delivery, timing of courses have all established norms in each client group and member state. The content of a course may be excellent, but delivered in the wrong style it can prove to be disastrous.

Clients of vocational education should always feel that what they are buying has been tailored to their specific needs. At the very least this means that student notes should bear a rubric dedicated to the client, while at the other end of the scale tightly tailored courses or programmes of study designed specifically to the needs of the mainland European client might be developed based on a previously successful UK model. Within this context it must be recognized that in future many clients may find the most appropriate and effective updating and retraining available to meet their needs on mainland Europe. This may result from differing technologies, research priorities or industry types in each member state. This both intensifies the marketing need for each institution actively to promote its educational and training products and services in the new markets that are opened up, and the value of international networking arrangements.

Clearly many higher educational institutions are networked across Europe through UETPs (University/Enterprise Training Partnerships), yet in further education this is uncommon. While it is true that many colleges have links with EC counterparts for exchange programmes, only recently have we seen active links promoting the teaching of modules overseas, in either the mother tongue or host country language; the offering of dual qualifications; links at LEA as well as institutional level; and the transnational bidding for European funding. All these activities require genuine networks across two or preferably more member states ideally linking the relatively 'affluent north' with the relatively 'underprivileged' south which is the current major priority area for EC structural funds.

The development of successful network arrangements takes time and this needs to be recognized when short- and medium-term goals are being set. The staff involved need clear managerial and professional lines of support. Student exchange programmes, particularly where students stay in the homes of their hosts, build friendships and create cultural awareness. However the responsibility for the well-being of individual students needs to be carefully considered and institutions, and where appropriate LEAs, need to develop clear procedures and action guidelines before such exchanges are undertaken. 'Home stay' arrangements can be cost-saving and exchanges with institutions in capital cities can be expensive. College years and examination times across Europe do not always coincide and can create problems for exchange programmes. The difficulties associated with a one-hour time difference and different bank holiday dates become less important in comparison.

The funding of such exchange programmes also need careful consideration. Options include: EC sources, the LEA, the institution's own budget, and student self-funding. However, despite the potential problems student exchanges are often a first step in building international links. They are useful in providing, in addition to their prime function, staff development and cultural awareness.

Finally, experience demonstrates that private sector vocational education providers and trade associations can be valuable sources of students and ideas. International companies are often the key to unlock the doors of new countries. For example, providing language training for the UK base or subsidiary of a multi-national company can lead to total immersion courses for mainland-based employees needing English language skills.

A growing market

In all cases the market for vocational education is changing and growing at an enormous rate. On November 4 1989 I left the UK for West Berlin not thinking for a minute that by the time I returned the following weekend the course of history would have changed so dramatically and that our market would have developed, in reality, to encompass East Germany. Since that date we have seen radical and far-reaching changes in Eastern Europe, with the EC and the UK Government pledging significant resources to aid Poland, Hungary, Romania and others. The opportunities are there: what is needed now is vision and not inward-looking, reflective management styles. The Single European Market is with us whether we like it or not. We must think and behave like Europeans.

PART IV

Predicting the Future

13 2002: Vocational Education in an Open Europe

The South East Essex
College of Arts & Technology
Carnarvon Road Southend on Sea Essex SS2 6LS
Tel: Southend (0702) 220400   Fax: Southend (0702) 432320

The Single European Market and vocational education – a summary

This book has stressed the importance of the implications of the Single European Market for vocational education in the UK, and indeed across the EC. The Single European Market will create new, and enhance existing, demands on vocational education. It will be for institutions to meet these demands if they are to fulfil their responsibilities to their community and maintain their own financial viability in the increasingly commercial practice of vocational education. Equally it has been argued that the economic future of the UK will largely depend on the competence and capability of its work-force. This places vocational education at the centre of a set of social policies designed to support and promote economic progress.

This economic imperative need not however contradict a set of educational values which place the learner at the centre of the learning process. Indeed it is argued in Part Two of this text that the divergent philosophies underpinning education and training are merging in a form of liberal vocationalism which recognizes the significance of a range of core interpersonal skills and learner empowerment to support the development of a 'world class work-force'. Within this overarching view the major requirement becomes one of offering enhanced Europeanized learning opportunities to the range of clients and segmented markets served by vocational education. While initiatives at EC, national, regional and local levels may be enormously supportive it is at the level of individual institutions that these enhanced opportunities can be offered. Critically then it is at this level of vocational educational activity that the challenge of Europe must be faced.

A model for enhancing Europeanized learning opportunities is offered in Chapter 3. This focuses on the interacting dimensions of: the curriculum; the culture, structure and processes of the institution together with its strategic and operational management; and the human resource available to it. A suggested strategy to empower the learner through a curriculum framework is mirrored by a similar approach to the empowerment of staff within the context of a clear institutional mission. Such empowerment supports the development of a 'love of change' although the importance of leadership in creating the required culture for change is stressed.

The Single European Market will generate new client expectations that UK institutions meet the best quality standards offered by competitor institutions on mainland Europe. The comparability and mutual recognition of qualifications will lead to a greater number of learning programmes offering transnational accreditation and workplace or study experience in one or more member states. The mobility of students will affect the recruitment policies of institutions and inevitably the curriculum they offer. However it is how the implications of the Single European Market are experienced within given localities which will primarily determine the nature and extent of the changed pattern of demand experienced by institutions. A significant increase in PICKUP-type provision, and vocational education for non-traditional groups, can be confidently predicted throughout the early 1990s unless such demands are significantly constrained by economic recession. However, despite this, skill shortages will persist throughout the 1990s, placing an employment premium on individuals with them. Future labour mobility across national boundaries is certain to be significantly concentrated among such individuals.

Predicting the future – 1992, ten years on

There can be little doubt that the vocational education system existing in the year 2002 will mirror the enormous changes likely to have occurred within Europe by that time. As outlined by Luff (in this text) the intention of the architects of the EC was to go beyond a single trading market to create forms of social, economic and political union in Europe based on a recognition of national interest but at the cost of national sovereignty.

We must build a kind of United States of Europe. (Churchill, 1946)

Prosperity and vital social progress will remain illusive until the nations of Europe form a federation of a 'European entity' which will force them into a single economic unit . . . Our concern is a solution to the European problem. (Monnet, 1943)

We are not forming coalitions between States, but union among people. (Monnet, 1978)

While the path towards European union was laid decades before factors such as perestroika in the Soviet Union, the democratization of the nations of Eastern Europe and concerns about the economic power of Pacific Basin states have led to the articulation of a set of powerful arguments supporting forms of union beyond that envisaged by the Single Economic Act. This has been most explicit in the outcomes of the Strasbourg European Council meeting of December 1989 which both supported the Social Charter (with the exception of the UK) but also supported a quickening pace towards other forms of union. An official publication from the Office of Official Publications of the European Community published after the Strasbourg European Council makes this clear:

A frontier-free Community in 1993, a financial Community from 1 June 1990, a monetary Community when the intergovernmental conference has completed its work – its duty now is to become to an even greater degree a Community in which democracy flourishes and the will of the people is paramount. When the Community Charter of fundamental social rights adopted in Strasbourg is put into practice, its effect must be to harmonize workers' individual and collective rights while consolidating those they have already won. And increasing the powers of the European Parliament is seen as a natural concomitant of the widening of the Community institutions' areas of jurisdiction, to offset the loss of powers of scrutiny which disturbs national parliaments as more and more of the legislation adopted is drafted in Brussels. The process of reform decided on in Strasbourg, then, must not be confined merely to the technical aspects of the economic and monetary union. If it is to be a full and legitimate reform, it must include the democratic checks and balances needed to ensure that the new mechanisms of power are monitored and encouraged by popular representation. What makes the expression of the people's will a still more vital feature of the reform is that the Commission itself is asserting its executive authority in a structure of federal lines and with federal powers. (Fontaine, 1990, p. 40)

Greater economic social and political union on the timescales considered following the Strasbourg European Council would have enormous implications, and create substantial opportunities, for vocational education. By 2002 it is possible to envisage legislation promoting equality of access to vocational education across the EC irrespective of race, gender, disability or place. This would have enormous resource implications given the traditional underprovision of vocational education in the UK by European standards. While it is unlikely that measures will be introduced by 2002 to fully harmonize vocational education provision across the EC it is likely that harmonization measures will be introduced in areas of curriculum design, quality assurance and assessment procedures.

It is possible to envisage legislation introducing a compulsory levy for vocational education on employers in the UK, following the German model. This would be in recognition of the large-scale investment in vocational education required, not least in information and communications technologies, to meet the challenges of the twenty-first century and the fulfilment of what Rajan terms the Second Industrial Revolution, one in which 'work skills and know-how have been emerging as a prime resource' (Rajan, 1990, p. 253).

Two factors emerge strongly from this analysis. First that just as the Single European Market will have significant implications for vocational education so too will the emerging patterns of economic, social and political union within the EC. This reinforces the view that change will remain an endemic factor within vocational education. The second point is that the lesson learnt from the unprecedented changes which occurred in Eastern Europe during 1989 is that change within the European arena is unpredictable. New markets and new opportunities will emerge for institutions offering vocational education on a new international basis in the future. It will be the pro-active, entrepreneurial institutions which take advantage of these opportunities and which grow to offer quality experiences for learners and staff alike.

References

Churchill, W (1946) Speech in Zurich 19 September, quoted in J M and M J Cohen (1980) *The Penguin Dictionary of Modern Quotations*, Penguin, Middlesex

Fontaine, P (1990) *Europe – A Fresh Start*, Office of Official Publication of the European Communities, Luxembourg

Monnet, J (1943) Extract from a note dated 5 August 1943, quoted in P Fontaine (1988) *Jean Monnet, a grand design for Europe*, Office of Official Publication of the European Communities, Luxembourg

Monnet, J (1978) *Memoirs*, Collins, London

Rajan, A (1990) *1992: A Zero Sum Game*, Industrial Society Press, London

Index